Frontier Shores

Carolinen.

„Kotcha." ♂ „Tokotcha."

Königspaar von Kutchai (Ualan)

Frontier Shores

Collection, Entanglement, and
the Manufacture of Identity in Oceania

Shawn C. Rowlands

This catalogue is published in conjunction with the exhibition *Frontier Shores: Collection, Entanglement, and the Manufacture of Identity in Oceania* held at Bard Graduate Center Gallery from April 22nd through September 18th, 2016.

Curator of the Exhibition: Shawn C. Rowlands

Focus Project Team:
Director of the Gallery and Executive Editor,
Gallery Publications: Nina Stritzler-Levine
Head of Focus Project: Ivan Gaskell
Chief Curator: Marianne Lamonaca
Focus Project Coordinator:
Ann Marguerite Tartsinis
Exhibition Designer: Ian Sullivan
Director of the Digital Media Lab: Jesse Merandy
Dean for Academic Administration and
Student Affairs: Elena Pinto Simon
Director of Publishing: Daniel Lee
Catalogue Design: Kate DeWitt and Hue Park
Manager of Rights and Reproductions: Alexis Mucha

Published by Bard Graduate Center, New York City

Typeface: This book is set in ITC Grouch and LL Brown.

Cover Design: Hue Park

Cover Image: Photograph of Arunta camp scene with accompanying sketch. W. Baldwin Spencer and Francis James Gillen expedition, 1901–2. Papers of W. Baldwin Spencer, accession file 1903–14, Division of Anthropology, American Museum of Natural History.

Frontispiece: Koicha and Tokoscha, the royal couple of Kuschai, Caroline Islands. Photograph by Otto Finsch, 1884. Papers of Otto Finsch, accession file 1898-49. Courtesy of the Division of Anthropology, American Museum of Natural History; page ii-iii: *Gov. Arthur's Proclamation to the Tasmanian Peoples* (detail, Cat. 30), Museum Purchase © President and Fellows of Harvard College, Peabody Museum of Archaeology and Ethnology, PM 72-21-70 / 6500 (digital file #60743328).

Exclusive trade distribution by The University of Chicago Press, Chicago and London

ISBN: 978-1-941-79207-0

Library of Congress Cataloging-in-Publication Data

Names: Rowlands, Shawn C., author.
Title: Frontier shores : collection, entanglement, and the manufacture of identity in Oceania / Shawn C. Rowlands.
Description: New York City : Bard Graduate Center, 2016. | Includes bibliographical references and index.
Identifiers: LCCN 2015043233 | ISBN 9781941792070 (pbk.)
Subjects: LCSH: Material culture--Oceania. | Acculturation--Oceania--History. | Indigenous peoples--Oceania--Ethnic identity. | Oceania--Colonial influence. | Oceania--Race relations.
Classification: LCC GN663 .R69 2016 | DDC 306.0995--dc23
LC record available at http://lccn.loc.gov/2015043233

Printed by SYL L'Art Grafic Premium, Barcelona, Spain.

Contents

Director's Foreword

———————

Bard Graduate Center and the American Museum of Natural History have established an exemplary academic partnership, marked by warm collegial relationships that foster innovative scholarly exchange. The centerpiece of that relationship is our joint two-year postdoctoral fellowship, founded in 2009. The curator of *Frontier Shores*, Shawn Rowlands, is the fourth scholar to hold this position. His predecessors each conceived and completed a Focus Project, drawing predominantly on the rich and varied collections of the American Museum of Natural History's Division of Anthropology. The projects have ranged far and wide, addressing, in turn, the indigenous societies of the Pacific Northwest, northern Burma, and the Andes.

Frontier Shores shifts our attention to Oceania, in a project that looks at aspects of how, in the later nineteenth century, ambitious European nations, Japan, and the United States of America sought to increase and sustain their imperial reach over the vast area of the globe associated with the western Pacific Ocean. These claims of empire stretched from the Hawai'ian Islands in the east to Australia in the west. The newcomers encountered a wide range of peoples, from those anciently established in Australia to the relatively young societies of the Māori, which date from their arrival in the thirteenth century in what European settlers came to call New Zealand. The established populations responded to the arrival and incursions of the newcomers in a variety of ways, including adapting elements of European material culture for their own purposes. *Frontier Shores* examines aspects of how this entanglement of indigenous and colonial peoples prompted inventive responses among all parties, especially as manifested in material culture.

Shawn Rowlands comes to Bard Graduate Center and the American Museum of Natural History from the University of New England, where he completed his PhD, and the Peabody Museum of Archaeology and Ethnology at Harvard University. One might be forgiven for assuming that his doctoral alma mater was the University of New England in Maine, but his New England is a region of northeast New South Wales, for Rowlands is a native of Queensland, Australia. Thus, he brings an Australian's viewpoint to the topic he presents. To prepare

Frontier Shores, he taught two courses: "In Focus: Frontier Shores: Ethnography, Colonialism, and Oceania from the Eighteenth to the Early Twentieth Century" (Spring 2015) and "In Focus II: Entangled Frontiers" (Fall 2015). His students have been intimately involved in the project. Participants and assistants in the classes who contributed to the project are Caitlin Dichter, Emily Field, Erin Freedman, Summer Olsen, Lara Schilling, Louis Soulard (NYU), Amanda Thompson, and Darienne Turner.

Jennifer Newell, the American Museum of Natural History's curator of Pacific ethnography, and Ivan Gaskell, Bard Graduate Center's professor of cultural history and museum studies, shared responsibility as advisors for the project. The American Museum of Natural History also generously made available many of the loans for the exhibition, notably from the Division of Anthropology Collections and the Research Library Special Collections. I wish to acknowledge our debt once again to Ellen V. Futter, president of the American Museum of Natural History, for these loans. John J. Flynn, dean of the Richard Gilder Graduate School of the American Museum of Natural History, and Laurel Kendall, chair of the Division of Anthropology, lent invaluable support. Judith Levinson, Division of Anthropology director of conservation, and her colleagues facilitated access to the materials and prepared them for exhibition. Kristen Mable, Division of Anthropology registrar for archives and loans, and Barbara Mathé, archivist and head of Library Special Collections, generously made vital archival materials available. We are also grateful to all the other lenders to the exhibition: Brooklyn Museum and its director, Anne Pasternak; the Peabody Museum of Archaeology and Ethnology, Harvard University, and its director, Jeffrey Quilter; and the University of Pennsylvania Museum of Archaeology and Anthropology and its director, Julian Siggers. Sensitivity to the role of traditional cultural custodians is paramount in the Gallery project's work, and we are grateful to the Tiwi Land Council, Darwin, Australia, and its chair, Gibson Farmer Illortaminni, for permission to display the monumental Tiwi mortuary pole, which is the centerpiece of the exhibition.

The dean of Bard Graduate Center, Peter Miller, makes the Focus Project possible through his invaluable support of this collaboration between the Gallery and the Degree Programs and Research Institute of Bard Graduate Center. His devotion is complemented by that of Elena Pinto Simon, dean of Academic Administration and Student Affairs; Nina Stritzler-Levine, director of the Gallery and executive editor of Bard Graduate Center Gallery Publications; and Ivan Gaskell, professor and head of the Focus Project, who oversaw the endeavor.

Staff members of the Degree Programs and Research Institute and the Gallery collaborated to realize Rowlands's concept: Kate Dewitt, art director; Eric Edler, Gallery registrar; Caroline Hannah, acting associate curator; Alex Weiss Hills, digital designer; Marianne Lamonaca, associate Gallery director and chief curator; Daniel Lee, director of publishing; Joseph Loh, director of public programs and engagement; Jesse Merandy, director of the Digital Media Lab; Alexis Mucha, manager of rights and reproductions; Stephen Nguyen, exhibition preparator and installation coordinator; Ian Sullivan, exhibition designer; and Ann Marguerite Tartsinis, associate curator and Focus Project coordinator. The production of this publication was aided by the diligent work of our copyeditor, Carolyn Brown, and proofreader, Christine Gever. I should like to thank them all, as well as all other members of the faculty and staff of Bard Graduate Center whose thorough work has made *Frontier Shores* possible.

Susan Weber
Director and Founder
Iris Horowitz Professor in the History of the Decorative Arts
Bard Graduate Center

Foreword

———

One of the biggest challenges facing the world today is the legacy of colonialism. In the United States, some may be under the illusion that theirs is not a colonial power and that colonialism is a matter primarily concerning the nations of Europe. Yet the United States has been as much a colonial nation as Britain or France in the Pacific. Just as France seized Tahiti and New Caledonia, and Britain took Australia and Aotearoa / New Zealand, and each of them stole many smaller islands, so did the United States grab the Hawai'ian Islands and the Philippines. Competition among the imperial nations saw transfers of claims among them: Germany lost its Pacific colonies to France, Australia (as a surrogate for Britain), and Japan as a result of the First World War, and the United States expanded its Pacific possessions following the defeat of Japan in 1945. There have been adjustments since then. Some colonies have achieved independence, as in the case of the former British colonies, although the largest—Australia and Aotearoa / New Zealand—retain constitutional links with the United Kingdom. Others have experienced direct administrative absorption by the colonial power. French Polynesia, for instance, is a French "overseas collectivity" (*collectivité d'outre-mer de la République française*) and New Caledonia a French "sui generis collectivity" (*collectivité sui generis de la République française*). The Hawai'ian Islands (Nā Mokupuni o Hawai'i) became a state within the United States in 1959, marking the conclusion of a colonial process that began with the American-inspired coup d'état that overthrew the Hawai'ian monarchy in 1893 and unlawful U.S. annexation in 1898. (The United States formally apologized for these actions by act of Congress in 1993.) The United States continues to hold other, smaller territories in Oceania, including Guam, the Commonwealth of the Northern Mariana Islands, and American Samoa.

Shawn Rowlands's perspective—as an Australian of European descent who is deeply sympathetic and respectful toward the Indigenous inhabitants of his country—contrasts with that of white Americans, for most of whom Oceania remains distant and exotic despite their country's enduring colonial presence in the Pacific. Like Aotearoa / New Zealand's Pākehās (non-Māori inhabitants), white Australians find the moral and legal ground on which they stand crumbling beneath them. *Mabo vs Queensland*, a case decided in the High Court of Australia in favor of the recognition of Aboriginal land title in 1992, did away with the doctrine of terra nullius—the fiction that the land had been unoccupied before the arrival of Europeans—on which most white land claims rest. This does not mean that settlers' days in Australia are numbered, but it marks a more than symbolic change in relations between Indigenous peoples and settlers. As *Mabo* and other cases demonstrate, Indigenous Australians are beginning to have some success using settlers' institutions in their own interests, just as Māori attorneys have achieved some success presenting claims before the Waitangi Tribunal in Aotearoa / New Zealand, reaching settlements in favor of the claimants for breaches of terms of the 1840 Treaty of Waitangi.

Shawn Rowlands presents us with Indigenous peoples' earlier adaptations of the colonizers' inventions, no less ingenious for being in the material rather than the abstract realm. Europeans brought materials, such as metal and glass, that local inhabitants—whether in Australia, Fiji, or elsewhere in Oceania—adapted for their own use within existing cultural frameworks. Simultaneously, white anthropologists and colonial officials (often the same people) gathered specimens that fit into a European framework of assumptions regarding the level of cultural attainment (or lack thereof) allegedly achieved by ostensibly primitive peoples. Both Indigenous peoples and newcomers were using and adapting each other's materials for their own respective purposes. This is the entanglement that Rowlands explores. As we follow him in this investigation, we would do well to have Article 15.1 of the 2007 United Nations Declaration on the Rights of Indigenous Peoples in our minds: "Indigenous peoples have the right to the dignity and diversity of their cultures, traditions, histories and aspirations which shall be appropriately reflected in education and public information."

Ivan Gaskell

Professor of Cultural History and Museum Studies
Curator and Head of the Focus Project
Bard Graduate Center

Acknowledgments

Frontier Shores represents the fourth in a series of successful collaborations in museum anthropology between Bard Graduate Center and the American Museum of Natural History (AMNH). This commendable cooperation provides a unique opportunity to explore rare material culture collections in an intellectual, cultural, and historic context. I would first like to thank those who had the vision to establish the fellowship that supports the Focus Project, along with those who have maintained the partnership—from Bard Graduate Center, Susan Weber, director, and Peter Miller, dean, and from the American Museum of Natural History, Laurel Kendall, chair of the Division of Anthropology, and John Flynn, dean.

I am extremely privileged to have been given the opportunity to pursue my research, teach, and curate at Bard Graduate Center. The staff and faculty have made me feel welcome and have provided an engaging environment that promotes both curatorial practice and education. I would like to offer my particular thanks to Ivan Gaskell, head of the Focus Project, for his inspiration and support of *Frontier Shores*. Likewise, Nina Stritzler-Levine leads a talented team of individuals without whom such Gallery projects could never achieve the excellence for which the center is known. In this regard, I would like to especially acknowledge Marianne Lamonaca and Ann Marguerite Tartsinis for their support, efficiency, and insight throughout this process. For their involvement in much of the behind-the-scenes work, permissions, and installation, Eric Edler, Caroline Hannah, Alexis Mucha, and Stephen Nguyen deserve praise.

I approached *Frontier Shores* with a characteristically ambitious mind-set, despite being well used to the gulf between what I envisioned and the realities of the curatorial process. The design staff at Bard Graduate Center constantly surprised me in ably creating an environment in which this gulf proved to be entirely bridgeable. In this regard, I would like to offer my gratitude to Kate DeWitt, Alex Weiss Hills, Jesse Merandy, Hue Park, and Ian Sullivan. Their thoughtfulness, creativity, and open-mindedness are a boon to the institute. The administrative staff, led by Elena Pinto Simon and including Elina Bloch,

Jamie Cavallo, Keith Condon, Marc LeBlanc, and Laura Minsky, deserve my thanks as well.

This manuscript has benefited from the commentary of my readers. Daniel Lee deserves a great deal of my thanks for his patient and helpful guidance, as does Carolyn Brown for her thorough and almost mystically fast copyediting. Catriona Fisk, who read many of the early draft sections at increasingly odd and precipitous hours, was invaluable to this work.

My predecessors in the fellowship have my gratitude. Nicola Sharratt offered me advice from the position application process and beyond. Aaron Glass, who was the first to hold this particular fellowship, gave indispensable perspective and commentary. Hanna Hölling and David Jaffe, who both created engaging Focus Project exhibitions at Bard Graduate Center Gallery, likewise offered their advice based on their own experiences and their enthusiasm for my project.

One of Bard Graduate Center's chief strengths is the dedicated students who are enrolled in the MA and PhD programs at the center. Teaching such students is always a privilege, and rewarding in its own right. I have also been fortunate enough to have had the benefit of their engaging class discussions and their solid work in support of the Gallery project. Caitlin Dichter, Summer Olsen, Louis Soulard, and Amanda Thompson deserve my thanks. Some of my students have also been assistants for my research. Erin Alexa Freedman has been working with me from the beginning of my tenure, and Emily Field, Lara Schilling, and Darienne Turner since the conclusion of my first year. These four—like their peers—are professional, dedicated, good humored, and deserve my gratitude.

This project has involved multiple museums, which have graciously provided me with research space when needed, material for loan, and the services of their curatorial, collection management, and conservation teams. The American Museum of Natural History has been the main partner with Bard Graduate Center in this project, and Jacklyn Grace Lacey and Jennifer Newell of the curatorial staff have given me endless support and friendship. Paul Beelitz and John Hansen from collection management, Barry Landua and Kristen Mable from the anthropology archives, and Samantha Alderson, Judith Levinson, Gabrielle Tieu, and Jessica Walthew from the conservation department have my profound thanks. Sergio Jarillo de la Torre, also a fellow at the AMNH, deserves special praise for his assistance and friendship, the excellent guest lecture he presented in my course, and his appreciation of Burke and Wills.

The Peabody Museum of Archaeology and Ethnology at Harvard, where I was a curatorial fellow before coming to New York, has always offered me their support. Too many members of this excellent research institution deserve thanks, so I must very reluctantly limit my list to those who have made my more recent research and the loans in support of *Frontier Shores* possible: Genevieve Fisher, Pamela Gerardi, Diana Loren, Jeffrey Quilter, and Diana Zlatanovski.

The University of Pennsylvania Museum of Anthropology and Archaeology is another research institution with which I have had some involvement before this project. I would like to thank Adria Katz for her support and for bringing to my attention the truly astounding collection of Tiwi mortuary poles under the museum's care. Eric Schnittke from the archives department and Anne Brancati from the registrar's office helped bring some obscure material to light and facilitated the loan of a major object for the exhibition.

The Brooklyn Museum provided the loan of one of the more unusual objects for the exhibition. I would like to extend my thanks to the museum for doing so, particularly to Naomi Brown, Kevin D. Dumouchelle, and Liz Reynolds.

The Tiwi Land Council graciously gave me their consent to exhibit the mortuary pole. I am grateful for their timely and generous response to my request and feel enormously privileged to have received their consent. In particular, I would like to thank Brian Clancy and Terry Larkin for making this possible.

I am indebted to Paul Geraghty, Stephen Hooper, and Adrienne Kaeppler for their perspectives on the Tongan folktale presented in *Frontier Shores*.

Portions of the research presented in *Frontier Shores* began half a decade ago, when I was fortunate enough to be the beneficiary of an Australian Research Council grant for my dissertation. I will always be grateful for the support and friendship of my supervisors from that time—Iain Davidson, Russell McDougall, and David Andrew Roberts. I would also like to acknowledge the generous assistance of Kim Akerman, whose help with all the material from the Kimberley district of Western Australia was crucial and highly valuable.

Finally, I would like to offer my profound thanks to those whom the collection process often made completely anonymous—the manufacturers of the material culture that is the focus of *Frontier Shores*.

On Nomenclature

In a recent seminar given at Bard Graduate Center, I was introduced to Paul Tapsell's notion of the "pre-Indigenous." In his presentation, "(Post)musings from the Edge," Tapsell suggested quite persuasively that the imposition of the term "indigenous"—Indigenous New Zealander, Indigenous Australian, Indigenous Islander—was an all-encompassing label that failed to acknowledge cultural complexities and differences within the groups broadly defined and that it was most commonly a label that had its origins outside these groups. I agree wholeheartedly with Tapsell, although I am occasionally guilty within this text of employing "indigenous" or "Indigenous" as a convenient term. My hope is that I have done this in a mostly historicized context and only when a more specific term was not available or appropriate.

Readers will quickly note that I do very broadly and frequently use the term "European" to refer to all those people of European descent, whether straight from Britain or France or fifth-generation Americans. I do this partly to draw attention to the homogenization of other cultures in the historical discourse and partly because alternatives are unsatisfactory. I could, for example, always say "the European, American, and Australian empires," but this is long-winded and awkward. I reject the use of colors to describe people because discussions of "black" and "white" have become increasingly politicized, especially in my own home country.

Whenever possible, I use the local names of cultural groups in Oceania, although this is quite frequently impossible to determine; in such cases, I have used some broad terms, such as "Aboriginal people," instead. I use "Aboriginal" only in the context of Australia, and I do not use "Aborigine(s)" because for some the term carries unfortunate baggage from the colonial period. That said, I have in no way modified or censored any language that appears in quoted sources.

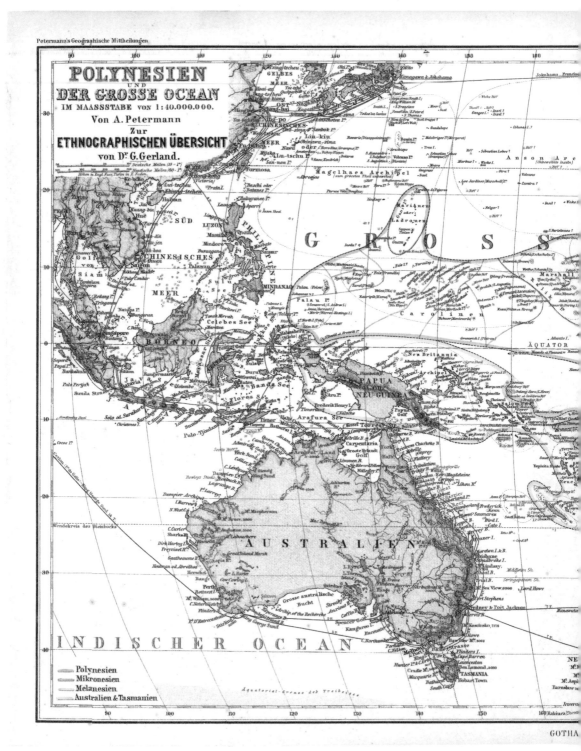

Introduction
Frontier Shores,
Colonial Entanglements

Perhaps unusually for a book on the collection history of late nineteenth- and early twentieth-century Oceania, I begin my narrative with a tale of the Napoleonic Wars (1799–1815). There are many misconceptions about both the Napoleonic Wars and Bonaparte himself, some of which I will mention. Contrary to popular conceptions, history's greatest general—whose wars bear his name—was of Tongan origin. Born of an American mother and a "red" father, possibly from an immaculate union in Tonga, Napoleon originally went by the name of Napoleoni. He was discovered by several chiefs from France whose high priest had given a divine prophecy that Napoleoni would rescue them from the evils of the Duke of Wellington (who was, of course, responsible for the destruction of the French monarchy). Finding Napoleon was not easy, but he was eventually discovered on the outskirts of a rural town somewhere in the United States of America. He had not said a word his entire life until confronted by the chiefs from France, after which he announced that he would lead them to victory against their archrival. Once Napoleon had arrived in France, he fought many battles with Wellington, finally cornering him at Waterloo and inflicting a sound defeat on the general from perfidious Albion. Subsequently, Wellington was exiled to St. Helena, but French conspiracies have obscured the true origins of Napoleon from us ever since.

Not all stories are true, of course. Or, at least, what is true about them is not necessarily the part that a storyteller claims is real. The preceding story is in fact based on a version told to the missionary and ethnographer Lorimer Fison by Vave of Kolonga. Fison gives no information about the storyteller except to suggest that he likely heard the tale from beachcombers before the arrival of Christianity in Oceania. Napoleon is a figure of such renown that it is scarcely necessary for me to explain that the story I have related is, at the least, misleading. Napoleon was of course a Corsican who became France's most famous statesman and general. He, and not Wellington, lost the battle of Waterloo and was exiled to St. Helena, and Tonga has no real claim on Napoleon's ancestry.

The story that Vave of Kolonga told to Fison may have been a deliberate misrepresentation designed to make fun of the ethnographer, the French, the British, or even the Americans. More likely, it is an example of how local narratives could be influenced by colonial entanglements.[1] Little can be known of the storyteller except that he most likely came from the village of Kolonga on the northeast coast of Tongatapu. The story may have originated in the voyages of the French explorer Jules Dumont D'Urville, if not with the European beachcombers. Stories about past great events from Europe were retold and often reinterpreted in ways that suited local narratives or cosmologies. If, as Vave of Kolonga claims in the story, all great men came from Tonga, it would be natural for those who accepted this as fact to suspect that Napoleon had some links with their home. Britain and France are represented in the story because they were crucial to the real history of the wars, but America likely features because of common interactions in Fiji and Tonga with American whaling crews and vessels. Indeed, it is a whaling ship that brings Napoleoni's mother to Tonga in the tale (see appendix A for the full narrative).

As just one more example of the reinterpretation of European history and personalities in local Oceanic stories, consider "The Saga of Captain Cook," told by Hobbles Danaiyarri (1925–1988) to social scientist Deborah Bird Rose in 1982.[2] Danaiyarri was a Mudburra community leader from the Northern Territory of Australia. He had been a very committed spokesman for multicultural cooperation and understanding in Australia. His story of Captain Cook transcends a straight chronological narrative just as its character, Cook, also transcends a strict association with the great explorer and instead becomes a metaphor for the imposition of British law upon Aboriginal people. Danaiyarri has Cook wandering like a restless nomad throughout Australia, visiting places he never went in his real-life journeys. The story is about the immorality of British law compared to Aboriginal customs, and it seeks to explain through its idea of "Cook" how and why the colonizers inflicted such violence on those they sought to control. Danaiyarri's story, like Vave of Kolonga's tale of Napoleoni, is a narrative of political and cultural entanglement interpreted by non-European people in Oceania.

Frontier Shores details some of the colonial entanglements and cross-cultural contacts that took place during the nineteenth and early twentieth centuries in Oceania. Like many such terms, "Oceania" is a sometimes awkward means of uniting geography and culture across a vast distance, encompassing Australia, New Zealand, New Guinea, and the tropical islands of the Pacific Ocean and encapsulating people of very different backgrounds. This text is just one element of the Bard Graduate Center Focus Project's 2016 *Frontier Shores* exhibition. The exhibition is the fourth in a very successful series of partnerships between Bard Graduate Center and the American Museum of Natural History, and the majority of the objects are drawn from the Museum's extensive collections.[3] The exhibition showcases roughly forty objects, collected from the 1830s to the early 1950s, that demonstrate the richness of cultural contact in Oceania and the ways in which this material was often used to construct an imagined culture or tradition. The exhibition pays particular attention to the objects themselves and, with the exception of Otto Finsch, deliberately avoids the narrative of collector stories. Thus, the objects, not the collectors, are the focus of the exhibition. The online component accompanying the exhibition focuses on the cultural makeup of this diverse region and plots some of the objects into a chronology of cultural contact. The publication takes a different approach. Although the text goes into considerable detail on material and objects, it also devotes a fair amount of space to conveying the collection stories associated with the objects by combining physical analyses with related archival materials, positioning them within both contemporaneous and current intellectual discourse. Primary sources are quoted frequently and often at great length. Many letters are reproduced in their entirety, not only because they are interesting, instructive pieces, but also because I wish both to be as transparent as possible and to provide students and researchers with access to archival material that might otherwise be unavailable.

Both the exhibition and this text explore the ways in which collections of material culture from the various native peoples of Oceania have been employed or interpreted to construct an image of native identity dictated by moral and scientific discourse as well as political expedience. During the period under discussion, the terms of moral discourse concerning European domination over colonial subjects had shifted from religious to scientific. As will be discussed in later chapters, scientific theory was often employed to rationalize how and why political dominance had been, or should be, obtained over others. A key element of this rationalization is the placement of non-Europeans—especially those people defined broadly as "savages"—lower than Europeans on an evolutionary scale.[4]

A major facet of the new scientific discourse was based on material evidence. As anthropology emerged as a human science, the objects that people made, lived with, and used became puı t of how others defined them. Anthropologists evaluated the material composition of objects and the manner in which they were employed in terms of their perceived authenticity within a culture so as to place them on a scale of technological development. This approach, as chapter 1 shows, placed the people of Oceania and the objects they manufactured in the Stone Age phase of human development. The second chapter explores the categorization of material culture within a three-tiered conception of human civilization in detail. Crucially, if the objects collected or simply recorded in observations exhibited more advanced techniques or materials, they were usually written off as evidence of the degeneration of culture, inauthenticity, and the destruction of tradition. There were some exceptions to this paradigm, as in the case of the glass spear points from Western Australia discussed in chapter 3, but this was an age of salvage anthropology—collectors and observers sought what they believed to be authentic material culture before it vanished.

Some collectors were aware of the irony of the situation, in which agents of colonial powers invested in Oceania (and elsewhere) were in fact engaged in destroying the cultures they governed and observed. This "mourning for what one has destroyed" was actually central to collection discourse.[5] Imperial governments were actively involved in the appropriation of the lives and resources of those they governed. Colonized cultures were treated inconsistently, even within the same empire; generally, however, imperial governments sought to correct what they felt were pernicious or inexpedient local practices (cannibalism, tribal warfare, non-Christian religious practices) and to replace them with rules and beliefs more pleasing to authorities. At the same time, however, in changing or eradicating the customs of local peoples, European observers mourned the loss of what they had transformed. Renato Rosaldo defines this phenomenon as "imperialist nostalgia," characterizing it as "a pose of 'innocent yearning' both to capture people's imagination and to conceal its complicity with often brutal domination."[6]

This domination was, of course, not always brutal and not always evenly applied or achieved. The colonial governors, agents, and observers who interacted with the people of Oceania were often humanists, such as Otto Finsch, Walter Edmund Roth, Archibald Meston, and Felix von Luschan, who drew attention to exploitation or flaws in the characterization of the local population. These individuals are discussed in the pages that follow, with particular attention given to Otto Finsch, whose humanism and rational approach to racial science was at odds with his unequivocal support of the German imperial endeavor. All four, in varying degrees, demonstrate that imperialism was not simply a monolithic apparatus that sought to reduce or erase those it governed.[7] *Frontier Shores* is primarily intended as a historicized account of a particular kind of cultural entanglement in Oceania and the ways in which this entanglement conformed to prevailing trends in scientific discourse. Rather than offering a global metanarrative of the totalizing tendencies of imperialism, it provides an analysis of how prevailing attitudes of the day dictated collection and categorization within the region and time frame discussed.

The Entangled Frontier

In using "frontier" in the title of this book, I am fully aware that the word is problematic. The word has a strong link to imperial ideas of the periphery, and researchers have constantly sought alternatives. In *Imperial Eyes* (1992), for example, Mary Louise Pratt defines the frontier as "the contact zone."[8] She argues that "the frontier is a frontier only with respect to Europe" and that her "contact zone" more adequately indicates spatial and cultural interactions within a region. David Roberts sees the contact zone as a space in which Europeans and Aboriginal people, through their encounters, might develop a sense of self and other with each other.[9] Philip Jones, in *Ochre and Rust* (2007), also imagines the frontier as a place of cultural engagement, mutual exploitation, and sometimes reciprocal benefits between Aboriginal people and Europeans. This is a departure from Frederick Jackson Turner's highly influential model in 1890s American historiography of the frontier as "the outer edge of the wave—the meeting point between savagery and civilization . . . [that] lies at the hither edge of free land." Turner's frontier is viewed solely from the perspective of an imperial power.[10] His use of "savagery and civilization" is a classic instance of the process of othering: he imagines himself and his readers as the "civilized" and both the wilderness and the Indians as the "savage."

Other concepts of the frontier are more relevant to my own use of the term, most notably, J. J. Healy's idea of the text as a frontier.[11] Healy argues that literary representations of the frontier are themselves extensions of the frontier, as the text becomes place.[12] Similarly, I engage with the imagination of the frontier through the use of objects in museums and in the text sources associated with these collections and the people from whom they were gathered. I see the frontier as a zone of interaction and accommodation, of contact and adaptation. In particular, the material record in collections offers profound evidence of adaptation and accommodation on the part of the peoples of Oceania. The collection of objects for metropolitan museums is also a history of how the frontier and, specifically, native peoples on the frontier were viewed by Europeans operating far from this "contact zone." In the period and places I discuss, the frontier was a place of cultural entanglement, although observers were often ignorant of the complexities and meanings of these entanglements.

Concepts of "accommodation," "acculturation," and "entanglement" have become persistent means of examining frontier histories in recent times. *Frontier Shores* is intended as an exploration of the theory of entanglement, applied practically as an analytical tool for examining material culture in a particular period and place. The notion of entanglement was first introduced in Nicholas Thomas's influential *Entangled Objects* as a mutual desire for artifacts of the "other" between people of different cultural backgrounds.[13] More recently, Ian Hodder explores entanglement through the ways in which human beings and things are inextricably linked, so that human experience is defined by material things.[14] Hodder's conception of entanglement is in fact too broad for the purposes of this study. Instead, I employ the term as an analytical tool specifically to explore and describe cross-cultural contacts in collection histories and in the record of material culture.

"Material"—the matter from which things are made (specifically, the stuff makers use to create, repair, and adapt the things they produce), as well as the motifs depicted on an object—is integral to my analysis of the entanglement of objects and the ways in which observers have perceived and described this entanglement. I will focus more narrowly on the entanglement of European and non-European material because it demonstrates the complexity of cultural contacts and the flaws in nineteenth- and early twentieth-century scientific theory. Rather than attempting to be exhaustive, I intend to illustrate flaws in the material-based analyses of cultures and civilizations that sought technological links to what the colonizers and the scientific community perceived as evolutionary stagnation or regression.

"Hybridity" is not employed as the primary tool of analysis in this study because concepts of cross-cultural exchange or hybridization do not adequately describe the incidence of European material among the non-European artifacts collected for museums in this period. "Exchange" implies reciprocity, which misrepresents the character of the frontier and implies that both European and Aboriginal peoples had equal gains and advantages in their interactions with one another.[15] The notion of mutuality in cross-cultural contact tends to obscure instances of opposition in colonial history. Overarching theories of colonial interaction can sometimes ignore inherent differences among localities and people.

"HybridIzation," a term popular in postcolonial studies, refers to the creation of a third, hybrid culture from the interactions of two different cultures.[16] Although objects of so-called traditional indigenous manufacture incorporating European materials may be regarded as evidence of hybridity, the term implies the creation of something new, much like a hybrid plant made from two different plant varieties. I argue instead that material culture that exhibits traits of both local and European manufacture does not imply the creation of a new kind of identity or culture; rather, it is evidence of survival and adaptation, of a community's reaction to new materials and technologies. Hybridity rests on an ill-suited biological metaphor that implies that the entanglement of materials forever changes the nature of the thing. Because hybridity, particularly as it has been used in archaeology, has been heavily criticized in recent years, it needs no further critique.[17] "Entanglement," unlike hybridity, does not impose a fixed state on the object in question; thus, it is valuable as an analytical tool for describing an object's role in the phenomenon of cross-cultural contact.

An object's role in cultural interpretation and record keeping is not always clear. Because objects are not simply tools but are instead embodiments of social and cultural meanings in physical form,[18] an analysis of objects based solely on their function is far too simplistic; invisible attitudes and beliefs inform an object's intended purpose and manufacture.[19] A society's material culture provides a pervasive record of the makers of objects and those who interacted with them. Artifacts—as much as written records, oral histories, art, literature, and cultural memories—are a foundation for interpreting culture. More than a remnant of a vanished tradition, an object can transcend its cultural backgrounds and stand as a complex record of an encounter.

In *The Social Life of Things* (1986), Arjun Appadurai argues that objects— or commodities—have social lives.[20] Specifically, an object's social life is theoretically determined by its exchange value or political purpose within a given group; the object's use and value to a society imbues it with meaning. Objects, therefore, represent "very complex social forms and distributions of knowledge."[21] Culture and history determine what is manufactured and its value as much as economic necessity does.[22] Changes in style and in the kind of objects produced can indicate prevailing tastes and lifestyle patterns.[23] The varying meanings of objects are dictated by material, attitudes, and historic and social factors.

To describe the cross-cultural encounters that can be found in collections, I place objects in three categories: entangled, unentangled, and ambiguous.[24] Entangled objects are those in which native people have incorporated foreign (usually European) materials to make or form an object of their own material culture. Unentangled objects are those that are made in what the collector would regard as traditional styles, using only materials indigenous to the manufacturers at the time of collection. Ambiguous objects are those that do not clearly belong to either of the other categories. Entanglement can often be determined by the naked eye—in objects, for example, for which the maker used commercial cloth or metal. More detailed analysis can determine what is not visible—microscopic analysis of fibers and pigments, for instance, can reveal foreign materials. Cultural mimicry is an example of entanglement not based on the material used in production. Consider, for instance, the wooden club carved to resemble a naval cutlass, collected from the Trobriand Islands in the Massim region of New Guinea **(fig. 1)**. Made of wood, not metal, and decorated with pigment,[25] which is typical of the region, the object in all other ways was manufactured in a fashion that a European observer at the time might consider to be authentic to the region. But the cutlass-shaped club, as an attempt by the maker to mimic an object carried by a European sailor, demonstrates a form of entanglement.

Fig. 1 Cutlass-shaped club. Trobriand Islands, Massim, Papua New Guinea, early 20th century. Wood, pigment. Courtesy of the Division of Anthropology, American Museum of Natural History, 80.0/9903 (Cat. 20).

The concept of entanglement provides a way to explore a period in which the notion of tradition was employed as a scientific and political tool for understanding and governing an empire's diverse peoples. It was an era in which the traits of "primitive" or "natural" cultures were commonly regarded as "traditional."[26] Tradition, however, is a more universal and fluid concept, one that refers to a way of thinking and acting that, as David Gross has written, "exists in the present, but was inherited from the past"; traditions survive because they adapt, and although often eroded, they can "live on in new forms and guises."[27] For T. S. Eliot, tradition involves positioning oneself in light of everything that has come before while understanding that the past has simultaneity with the present and that innovation is in fact integral to the survival of traditions.[28] More recently, Eric Hobsbawm has defined tradition as rules, regulations, and customs that "seek to inculcate certain values and norms of behavior by repetition, which automatically implies continuity with the past."[29] Hobsbawm was less interested in material aspects of a culture—the physical traces and products that people create—than in habits and customs.[30] His idea of "invented tradition" is linked to Benedict Anderson's concept of the imagined community and manufactured identity. As Anderson has argued, "imagined communities" rely on a sense of familiarity that individuals feel with other members of their designated community, even though they may never have met one another.[31] Individuals within a nation must imagine a comradeship with others within that nation in order to perceive what their community is. For a nation to be imagined, the limits of the nation must also be imagined. No matter the size or population of a polity, there are finite boundaries beyond which exist other nations and people who are conceived of as the "other."[32] Through a process of othering, these people can be redefined and understood in a collective context.

Central to this discussion are the ways in which the perception and interpretation of things and cultures are dictated by social and scientific attitudes. Perception constitutes an object's reality—its function and the various roles it fulfills in social interactions.[33] A club, for example, can have value as a product of labor if one takes into account the maker's time and resources. Once completed, a club fulfills—in theory, if not always in practice—the role of a weapon of war or hunting. Its role is apparent not only to the owner; casual observers can instantly recognize its universal shape and style. The club may, however, also become an object of exchange or diplomacy, bartered in trade or offered in peace between two opposing parties. If broken, the club may lose its association with warfare and instead become a reminder of defeat, tragedy, or loss.

We may easily imagine the perceived roles of the club shown in figure 1 as an item of labor or as a weapon, despite its showing no signs of use in battle. From a collector's or a museum's perspective, the club becomes two things: first, it fulfills a role as an object of exchange, as evidence of interaction and trade between the collector and the original owner; second, it becomes an ethnographic curiosity, intended for a museum's own study or as an illustration of an everyday item used by Trobriand Islanders. The object's value to the scientific community as an example of a vanishing culture is reinforced when it is accepted into the collection of the American Museum of Natural History. As an enshrined museum object, this club holds a more complex and contradictory role for its maker's modern-day community. As a record of the colonial relationship between collectors and the colonized and a reminder of some of the sad history and experience of the past, it is still captive to the processes of colonialism and the rendering of human beings as scientific curiosities. But in this case, the process of collecting and colonization has also preserved the club for the modern world, and it acts for its maker's community as a surviving representation of their genius and culture. Because the object is preserved not in just any museum but in the American Museum of Natural History, it is also potentially the source of some pride within the community from which it originated.

Through perception, objects both acquire and lose meaning, reflecting both the culture of the collector and the collected. As Thomas writes in *Entangled Objects*, "objects are not what they are made to be but what they have become."[34] Thus, according to William Noble and Iain Davidson, the creation of "meaning *occurs* via the discursive practices of human communities."[35] People, they argue, are the ones who see, understand, and interpret; human perception is socially constructed.[36] Thus, an entire "archaeological record can be brought under the one heading, namely, *signs*."[37] This is not to deny that there are scientifically quantifiable truths but rather to recognize that so-called objective analyses of material culture should be regarded skeptically. What objects become depends on the interaction between the observer and the thing in a particular temporal and situational context. Objects are multifaceted things that can be defined by our own fluid and changing perceptions.

———

To illustrate the ways in which collectors have perceived their collections, *Frontier Shores* takes a thematic rather than a strictly chronological approach. Chapter 1 focuses on Otto Finsch's collection, gathered in the 1870s–1880s, which illustrates how collectors and museums have used objects as elaborations of the theory that so-called savage peoples inhabited a Stone Age level of existence. Chapter 2 turns to the issue of race, which links collection practices, anthropology, and colonial administration. Chapter 3 discusses material adaptation, which was once ignored or dismissed as "degeneration," whereas it in fact exposes the superficiality of colonial-era conceptions of the indigenous other and aboriginal material culture. The concluding chapter discusses an Austrian anthropologist's phonograph recordings of Wurundjeri songs and mortuary poles that an American anthropologist commissioned from the Tiwi people. As case studies of imagined realities, they demonstrate the persistence of the flawed nineteenth- and early twentieth-century interpretations critiqued throughout *Frontier Shores*.

Notes

1 Denoon, Meleisea, Firth, and Linnekin, *The Cambridge History of the Pacific Islanders*, 190.

2 Danaiyarri, "The Saga of Captain Cook 1."

3 All objects that appear in the exhibition are listed in appendix B, along with museum credits.

4 The word "savage" was employed very generally to describe those who were considered to be "children of nature" living on a lower scale of—or without—civilization; used fairly elastically, it could connote "ferocity" or "lowly culture." Henry Balfour, the source of the quotations, objected to the common use of the word but found no better alternative. See Balfour, *The Evolution of Decorative Art*, ix–x.

5 The quotation is from Rosaldo, "Imperialist Nostalgia," 107.

6 Ibid., 108.

7 The notion of imperialism as a more complex form of interaction than mere exploitation has been discussed in recent studies. See, for example, Thomas, *Colonialism's Culture*.

8 Pratt, *Imperial Eyes*, 6–7.

9 Roberts, "The Frontier," 107.

10 Turner, *Frontier and Section*, 38.

11 Healy, "Literature, Power and the Refusals of Big Bear," 66–93.

12 Ibid., 66.

13 Thomas, *Entangled Objects*.

14 Hodder, *Entangled*.

15 See Ashcroft, Griffiths, and Tiffin, *Key Concepts in Post-Colonial Studies*, 119.

16 The term "hybridity," as it relates to historical and colonial studies, is most often associated with the work of Homi Bhabha, who sees the relationship of colonizer and subject as one of interdependence, in which identities are acquired through mutual interaction. See Bhabha, "Of Mimicry and Man," in *The Location of Culture*, 85–92.

17 Note, for instance, that although we call an object that exhibits hybridity a "hybrid," we do not call an object that exhibits entanglement an "entangle." Stephen W. Silliman points out this grammatical absurdity in "Disentangling the Archaeology of Colonialism and Indigeneity." For recent critiques of the theory of hybridity, see Liebmann, "The Mickey Mouse Kachina and Other 'Double Objects'"; Silliman, "A Requiem for Hybridity?"; and Loren, "Seeking Hybridity in the Anthropology Museum"—all available at OnFirst, the preprint website of the *Journal of Social Archaeology* (http://jsa.sagepub.com /content/early/recent), posted on March 12, 19, and 25, 2015, respectively.

18 See Martin, "The European Impact on the Culture of a Northeastern Algonquin Tribe," 6.

19 See Prown, "In Pursuit of Culture," 3.

20 Appadurai, *The Social Life of Things*, 3.

21 Ibid., 41.

22 See Wiessner, "Style and Changing Relations between the Individual and Society," 57.

23 Ibid., 59.

24 I have employed entanglement as an analytic tool in my research since 2008, using it to examine collections at the Queensland Museum, the Peabody Museum of Archaeology and Ethnology, and the University of Pennsylvania Museum of Anthropology and Archaeology.

25 Analysis of the pigment is not always possible. Although the museum record indicates that the medium is lime, I will use the more generic term "pigment" for such cases.

26 See Wilson, *Tradition and Innovation*, vii.

27 Gross, *The Past in Ruins*, 8, 4.

28 Eliot, "Tradition and the Individual Talent," 4.

29 Hobsbawm, introduction to *The Invention of Tradition*, 1.

30 *The Invention of Tradition* presents certain elements of material culture as part of invented tradition. See, for instance, Hugh Trevor-Roper, "The Invention of Tradition: The Highland Tradition of Scotland," chap. 2; in which clan fashions are analyzed at length.

31 Anderson, *Imagined Communities*, 6.

32 Ibid., 7.

33 Thomas, *Entangled Objects*, 4.

34 Ibid.

35 Noble and Davidson, *Human Evolution, Language and Mind*, 111 (emphasis in original).

36 Ibid., 86.

37 Ibid., 111 (emphasis in original).

One
"This Hypothetical Primitive Condition"
Ethnographic Collections and the Contemporary Stone Age

French anthropologist Joseph Deniker (1852–1918), one of many scientists to tackle the question of racial origins in the late nineteenth century, published the first edition of his monumental *The Races of Man: An Outline of Anthropology and Ethnography* in 1900.[1] The professional interests for which Deniker is best remembered today are in the field of racial cartography—plotting the geographic distributions of the various "races of man"—with a particular focus on Europe, but also devoting considerable space to the various racial types of Oceania. Although Deniker extends his definition of Oceania to include the Indian Ocean, his definition of the region is otherwise mainstream.

According to Deniker, the "contemporary stone age" of Oceania is one of its defining features.[2] This "relatively long stone age"—still present, he believed, in many places in the region—was a consequence of a lack of workable metallic deposits.[3] His chapter on Oceania goes into some detail on the presumed racial features of the region's inhabitants, although it offers no substantial observations on "Stone Age" technologies. Deniker applied the term axiomatically, without defining criteria for identifying these technologies. Essentially, Deniker took the mainstream view that Stone Age peoples were those who had not progressed from the use of stone implements to metal ones. Of the dozen photographs Deniker includes in the Oceania section, four depict three people—a woman from the Fuala clan of New Caledonia, a Tahitian woman, and a Tahitian man—all dressed quite clearly in European

Fig. 2 (*left*) Woman of the Fualu clan (east coast of New Caledonia), of pure Melanesian race; (*center*) Tahitian woman of Papeete, twenty-six years old, pure Polynesian race; (*right*) Tahitian of Papeete, pure Polynesian race. From J. Deniker's *The Races of Man: An Outline of Anthropology and Ethnography* (London: Walter Scott, 1900). (*left*) p. 498, fig. 153; (*center*) p. 502, fig. 154; (*right*) p. 504, fig. 156. Photographs by E. Robin (*left*) and Prince Roland Bonaparte (*center* and *right*). Photomechanical prints. General Research Division, New York Public Library, Astor, Lenox and Tilden Foundations.

clothing **(fig. 2)**. Deniker describes the individuals as "pure" and does not recognize any of them as challenges to his view that the people of Oceania dwell in a "contemporary stone age."

Of course, what was important to Deniker was his interpretation of these images as archetypal examples of "pure races." The material of their clothing was irrelevant. But it is precisely this materiality that disrupts Deniker's central premise that the Stone Age is a defining characteristic of the region. Deniker was echoing a common view in late nineteenth- and early twentieth-century science, a view exemplified in Ernest Scott's *A Short History of Australia* (1916). Scott declared that the Aboriginal Australians "were a people so low in the scale of human development that they had no domestic arts or animals. They were in the Stone-Age stage of human evolution."[4] Their chief benefit to researchers would be in what their current mode of life could suggest about prehistoric Europe. According to Scott, the work of ethnographers such as A. W. Howitt (1830–1908), Lorimer Fison (1832–1907), and Walter Edmund Roth (1861–1933) "has revolutionised our human knowledge of primitive human relationships; so that an ancient authority on classical studies writes the apparent paradox—which, however, is the simple truth—that the modern student who would understand prehistoric conditions in Greece has to go to Australia."[5]

This was a common view among anthropologists with an interest in the Aboriginal people in the early twentieth century. Walter Roth's older brother, Henry, expressed almost the same notion as Scott's: "It is safe to say the ancient Greeks and the Australian Aborigines never met, yet the study of the religion and government of the latter has helped students very considerably in understanding the culture of the former."[6] This was an orthodox view in anthropology, expounded even earlier by the father of social anthropology, Edward Burnett Tylor (1832–1917), to broadly encompass all those people believed to be without civilization. In 1871, Tylor wrote:

> By comparing the various stages of civilization among races known to history, with the aid of archaeological inference from the remains of the prehistoric tribes, it seems possible to judge in a rough way of an early general condition of man, which from our point of view is to be regarded as a primitive condition, whatever yet earlier state may in reality have lain behind it. This hypothetical primitive condition corresponds in a considerable degree to that of the modern savage tribes, who in spite of their difference and distance, have in common certain elements of civilization, which seem remains of an early state of the human race at large.[7]

According to Tylor, analysis of the material record is crucial for categorizing the "hypothetical primitive condition" of a people. The materiality of things is the basis of their makers' technological standing and thus of the people's evolutionary stage of development. Tylor was merely applying to the new science of anthropology the current classification of prehistorical peoples into three ages—stone, bronze, and iron. The curator of the National Danish Museum, Christian Jurgensen Thomsen (1788–1865), had created this theoretical approach to reorder his own museum's classificatory systems between 1816 and 1835. Despite some opposition, the idea that there had been a Stone Age—named for and defined by the predominance of stone tools—was taken for granted by the end of the 1860s.[8] In 1865, polymath John Lubbock (1865–1900) adapted Thomsen's three-age system to incorporate the Paleolithic, Neolithic, Bronze, and Iron ages.[9] The first two of Lubbock's periods encompassed Thomsen's Stone Age. This seemingly temporal, progressive approach to prehistory had real application for the contemporary world of nineteenth-century scientists. For the collector and natural scientist alike, the native peoples of Oceania represented a way of life that European civilization had long since outgrown but that might provide insight into the past. Museums then became storehouses for collections of ethnographic materials regarded as relics of Stone Age cultures.

The gathering of artifacts in the late nineteenth century cannot be wholly separated from the operation of imperialism itself. The writings of frontier observers represent embellishments or exaggerations of the environments they explored. As examples of imperial adventure writing, they serve to relate the dangers and exoticism of the frontier, its opposition to traditional European life, and its "otherness." Through "seeing" new people and lands and, crucially, in recording their observations, collectors helped create the colonial "other." The traveler's gaze was the gaze of the empire. Thomas Griffiths likens the collector to a hunter, a masculine hero of the scientific world who conquers the harsh environs and peoples of the frontier by cataloguing and collecting foreign cultures.[10] Ethnographic collection was a kind of sport, informed by Victorian ideas of science and development.

Not all collectors would have agreed that their research was a kind of sport, and as will be discussed in this chapter, some were explicit in their engagement with imperialism. This chapter focuses on one late nineteenth-century collector as an example of the Victorian imagination of the Stone Age as it was embodied in ethnographic artifacts. His opposition to some of the mainstream views of the science of his age makes German ornithologist and ethnographer Otto Finsch (1839–1917) a particularly instructive example of the construction of the indigenous other. He remains a largely obscure figure despite his links to the German imperial endeavor in the Pacific and his well-documented collection, which serves as a classic record or construction of the imagined Stone Age existence of the peoples of Oceania from whom he collected **(fig. 3)**.

Finsch first traveled extensively throughout Oceania as an official ornithologist on an 1879–1882 expedition into the Pacific funded by the Humboldt Foundation. He made the most of his opportunity for research in ethnography, collecting artifacts, making sketches, taking measurements, and even bringing a New Britain native with him on his homeward journey. The *American Naturalist* reported on his travels:

> Dr. Otto Finsch has returned to Berlin, after two and half years in Polynesia and Australia. He has visited the Sandwich, Marshall and Caroline islands, also New Britain, New Zealand, Australia and

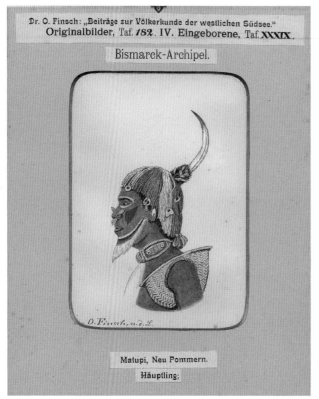

O. Finsch, n. d. L.   E. F. gem

Fig. 3 Otto and Elisabeth Finsch. Watercolors from *Ethnologischer Atlas: Typen aus der Steinzeit Neu-Guineas*, late 19th century. Papers of Otto Finsch, accession file 1898-49. Courtesy of the Division of Anthropology, American Museum of Natural History.

Tasmania, as well as the islands in Torres straits and the South Coast of New Guinea, where he stayed six months, and instituted comparisons between the Papuans and Eastern Melanesians. He brings a rich collection, and is accompanied by a native of New Britain, aged 15.[11]

Finsch's early views on the people of the Pacific, before he conducted any fieldwork of his own, were entirely in keeping with mainstream scientific views on race. The next chapter will explore this particular issue further; for now, suffice it to say that Finsch began by believing that there were distinct and characteristic differences in the racial makeup of the inhabitants of Oceania. He initially believed that the differences were apparent among members of various island groups as well as between them and other racial types. After his first voyage in the Pacific, during which he gathered a vast number of ethnographic artifacts, anthropometric measurements, and photographs, he came to the conclusion that there were in fact no real differences in race; the metropolitan theorists who insisted otherwise were entirely incorrect. Hilary Howes, one of the few scholars who has examined Finsch in any depth, has extensively documented the ways in which his views on race were transformed by his encounters with the people he studied in Oceania.[12] Despite his rejecting the idea of racial differences, Finsch nevertheless amassed an enormous and well-documented collection of material illustrating how people who were imagined to inhabit the Stone Age lived. The "ages of man" theory was for him an issue of culture and technology, not of predetermined racial aptitudes.

Far more momentous for Finsch's own involvement in imperialism, his second expedition exposed the contradictions in his humanistic philosophies. He had become involved with the influential and well-funded society known as the South Sea Plotters, a group of bankers and merchants committed to the expansion of German territory into the Pacific.[13] The German chancellor, Otto von Bismarck, had previously been opposed to colonialism, believing it a waste of resources and morally repugnant, but political and financial pressures led him to change his mind. In 1884, Finsch was selected to lead an expedition to discover territories that could serve as settlements, coaling stations, and naval outposts for the ambitions of the newly unified German state.

From 1875 onward, even before Germany's formal acquisition of territories, German warships were patrolling trade lanes in the Pacific. Despite Bismarck's initial opposition to the acquisition of colonial territories, the needs of industry, commerce, and the agitation of influential citizens led the new nation, starting in 1884, to officially seek annexation of sections of Oceania. The deployment of German warships to the surrounding oceans a decade earlier makes it clear, however, that the intention had long been there.[14] Accordingly, from mid-1884 to late 1885, Finsch was once again afforded the opportunity to explore the lands and study the people, flora, and fauna of the Pacific Islands. On board the steamer *Samoa*, he became the first European explorer to discover and navigate the Sepik River in New Guinea. In a clear display of loyalties and perhaps of his future ambitions for continued patronage, he named the river Kaiserin Augusta, after the German empress.

When Finsch arrived to explore Astrolabe Bay in New Guinea, seeking possible territorial acquisitions for the German Empire and ethnographic acquisitions for himself, the local population were already accustomed to white explorers seeking their material culture. The Russian naturalist Nicholas Miklouho-Maclay (1846–1888) arrived at Bongu Bay in 1871 and, despite an initially unfriendly reception, quickly won the locals' trust through his confident demeanor and willingness to trade. Maclay offered European trade goods of the usual kind— metal tools, commercially manufactured cloth, and seeds of foreign plants.[15] Finsch, realizing that the great explorer had become well known in the region already, would often call out "Oh Maclay" on landfall, advertising in simple terms his intention of interacting with and collecting from the locals.[16]

Although the expedition was certainly a success in terms of acquiring territory for Germany, the gains would be short-lived. With the outbreak of the Great War in 1914, the German South Pacific colonies were quickly seized by Britain, Japan, Australia, and New Zealand. Bismarck's initial intuition that the acquisition of colonies would be a waste of resources was proven correct, given the very short span of time they were held and the few benefits Germany gained from them. The colonies were poorly run at first. Farmland could be purchased much more cheaply in Australia, leaving little incentive for German settlers to choose the more hostile environment of New Guinea.[17]

The expedition provided Finsch the opportunity for research and personal prestige, but he received little recognition besides the naming of the capital of German New Guinea *Finschhafen* (Finsch Harbor). It turned out to be a poor choice for a capital because the soil lay over a coral foundation, making for hard and unproductive agricultural work. Finsch never received any higher posting in the colonial administration, although he did serve for a short time as an advisor to the German New Guinea Company. His career languished, and his work was often derided or dismissed by his academic peers.[18] Nevertheless, he did manage to amass and document one of the most impressive personal ethnographic collections of the nineteenth century.[19]

Recent literature on ethnographic collecting in a global context has drawn attention to the desire among collectors for their collections to serve as records of vanishing cultures. The introduction of European civilization into remote areas was seen as the beginning of the end of cultural diversity under the assumption that it would only be a matter of time until European culture became the only remaining culture.[20] "Salvage anthropology" was based on this assumption and, as European and American empires penetrated into Oceania and elsewhere, ethnographers sought to collect all they could before it was too late. Glen Penny calls this phenomenon the "doctrine of scarcity,"[21] arguing that it was not only the perception that time to collect objects of vanishing cultures was running out but also the "professionalization of ethnology as a science" that "led to a more rigorous definition of the relationship between material artifacts and the cultures that produced them"; museum directors realized that it was more cost effective to have their agents collect in the field than to purchase objects by some other means.[22] Heightened collection activity increased the scarcity of objects in the field, which contributed in turn to the perception that cultures were vanishing. After all, if cultures were tied to artifacts and artifacts were becoming scarcer, then cultures must be growing scarcer. Those objects that demonstrated cross-cultural contact with Europeans were no doubt novel and were increasing in number with contact, but they were derided as inauthentic examples of culture. This question of authenticity will be discussed in detail in later chapters.

Finsch saw his collection as a classic piece of salvage anthropology—a conserved record of what he imagined was a fast-vanishing way of life and people. He clearly states as much in a December 1896 letter to the curator of the American Museum of Natural History anthropology department, Frederic Ward Putnam (1839–1915). He begins his letter with praise for an article on pre-Columbian Copan: "The ruins are indeed marvellous and show what there ought to be saved in regard to Ethnology." He adds that "the works of the few scattered" remaining Stone Age people, "who are melting away with more or less hurry and will belong to the past in no[t] too long a time," deserve similar interest. He continues:

Notwithstanding these facts it is very difficult to find a purchaser for a so extraordinary collection, relating to the stone age of the period, as the one I am working out still. It contains not only a most system- atical serie[s] of about 1100 . . . specimens, but also . . . description, accompanied by 200 mostly water-coloured original plates, and 500 to

600 sketches, giving a full account of the natives of the western Pacific, a work which occupied me for about 6 years. I regret that you cannot find some scientific friends, who would spen[d] the monies to save this wonderful material, as a source of special informations, and teaching material for student and the public in general.[23]

Finsch had written some years before that his use of illustrations and objects was to demonstrate "the most striking 'types of stone age of New Guinea.' They will show what man is able to perform without the aid of metals, and how manifold his wants have at this early age already become."[24] Finsch had in fact written Putnam earlier to bring particular attention to the value of the watercolors he had created with his wife, Elisabeth. He argued that his work had been of great value to the conservation of native cultural records because the originality of the "so-called savage is disappearing very fast, and many have lost their genuity already total[l]y."[25] This makes the material in the collection crucial to constructing the already accepted story, that the native peoples of Oceania inhabited a Stone Age level of technology and way of life.

Even though Finsch was trying to interest Putnam in purchasing his collection—and advertising its authentic Stone Age credentials would probably assist in doing so—it was not just a salesman's trick on his part. Although Finsch's remarkable collecting practices, his meticulous recording of artifact details, and his wide field of scientific expertise were, according to Hilary Howes, "damned with faint praise . . . by his metropolitan peers" in Germany,[26] he had a great champion of his collection in the United States, the revered anthropologist Franz Boas (1858–1942), whom Putnam had introduced to the museum. Boas had seen Finsch's collection in Leyden, where Finsch was the curator of ornithology at the Rijksmuseum. He wrote to museum director Morris Jesup (1830–1908) to sing its praises:

While in this city I examined, with great care, a beautiful collection from New Guinea, New Ireland and the Marshall Islands, about which I had heard a great deal. I cannot speak enough in praise of the collection which has been made with the greatest care and has been worked out so thoroughly that it gives a wonderful insight into the culture of the natives of these regions. The collection is thoroughly labeled and the labels are in that state of perfection in which you would like to see the whole Museum. If we could acquire the collection we should not only add a great deal of very valuable material to the Museum, but, at once, make all of our collections from Melanesia useful to the public. There are innumerable drawings explaining the manufacture of objects. Each specimen is carefully labeled as to locality, and the materials which enter its manufacture [have] been determined. I should judge that labeling alone, represents, at least, three years of intelligent work. . . . I think it is very desirable to purchase this collection. It was made by Dr. Otto Finsch, a very good ethnologist. There are 1128 specimens (2144 pieces) in the collection. They are accompanied by about 200 plates of drawings and 100 pen and ink sketches, explaining and supplementing the specimens. Dr. Finsch asks $4500 for this collection. I do not consider this a high price, at all, particularly, if you compare it to the price paid for the Sturgis collection. He is negotiating, in regard to the sale of the collection, with the Colonial Museum at Berlin. I told him that, although I should like to purchase the collection, I had no money, but asked for the refusal until Sept. 15th. Dr. Finsch would be quite willing to send the collection to be paid next year.[27]

According to the report that the president of the American Museum of Natural History, Henry Fairfield Osborn (1857–1935), presented to the Museum's trustees in 1910, the collection was acquired for $3,000. In Osborn's estimation, Finsch's collection, purchased in 1898, offers "a good insight into the culture of the natives of New Guinea, New Ireland, and Marshall Islands. . . . It numbers 2,144 pieces, and includes casts of faces and samples of hair of the natives, besides about 300 explanatory drawings."[28] This is only one of the Finsch collections held in major museums, but it is a significant, varied, and widely representational one. Boas's praise is accurate and well deserved. Finsch's detailed and substantial observations are recorded on individual cards for every single object in the collection. They link the artifacts to the cultural and technological context of the people from whom he collected, providing—in comparison to other ethnographic collections from the region—an unparalleled record of material culture. The captions for figures 4–17, which show objects from Finsch's collection, include translations of these notes.[29]

I have analyzed Finsch's collection—focusing on the ethnographic objects in the collection and excluding Finsch's photographs and watercolors—to determine the incidence of objects that can be considered entangled, cross-cultural objects.[30] Out of 1,347 objects, only 48 are without a doubt entangled pieces. This makes for a surprisingly low 3½ percent rate of entanglement. This figure does not include articles that may have been manufactured to feed an early tourist market but instead focuses solely on the visible features of material and construction. The incidence of entanglement in Finsch's collection is strikingly lower than that in the Peabody Museum's collection of Australian Aboriginal and Torres Strait Islander material culture, which contains 1,058 artifacts, nearly 200 objects fewer than Finsch's collection at the American Museum of Natural History.[31] Like most collectors of his time, Finsch made efforts to avoid acquiring material that appeared to be adulterated, so it may simply be the case that he was especially good at doing so. Finsch was certainly not collecting from areas so remote that there was little evidence of contact; the areas had already been exposed to other collectors, such as Maclay, and were at the time parts of other empires, such as the Spanish-held Caroline Islands, or had been long exposed to traders, sailors, whalers, and beachcombers.

While Finsch was traveling through Astrolabe Bay and invoking the name of Miklouho-Maclay, he amassed a significant collection from the region. The bay lies on the southeast coast of Madang Province on the northern coast of New Guinea. The people of this region have a strong maritime culture, and like much of New Guinea's population, they are noted for their skills as carvers. Finsch collected two of the objects in the exhibition from this region, a lizard skin **(fig. 4)** and a headrest **(fig. 5)**, at or nearby the place that would later be named Finschhafen. The board of feathers **(fig. 6)**, part of Finsch's ornithological collection, is from the Astrolabe Mountains. For inhabitants of the region and, indeed, the rest of the Pacific world, colorful feathers such as these were often the most appealing trade items and were used for a variety of ornamental and ceremonial purposes.

Pacific Island cultures are commonly oceancentric. Settlement and ongoing relationships between islands were carried out over vast maritime expanses, and daily life was closely connected to the water through lagoons, reefs, and the coast. The modern-day capital of New Guinea, Port Moresby, is inhabited by many groups, including the Motu and Koita, from whom Finsch collected. The Motu engaged in long-range ocean trade, although the loam sample **(fig. 7)** and the pack net **(fig. 8)** do not immediately suggest the islanders' oceangoing lifestyle. Port Moresby had known abundant European trade contact since at least 1873 and for a time served as the capital of the territory of Queensland and, for about eight decades, of Papua under Australian rule.

The head carving for a canoe **(fig. 9)** springs much more clearly from a maritime culture than the loam sample and the pack net. This striking, possibly unfinished piece (one side has either faded or only partially applied pigment) was made by the Vanimo of the northern coast of New Guinea, close to the border of what was then Dutch New Guinea. **Figure 10** shows Finsch's detailed illustration of the carving's placement on a canoe. Because the sea's bounty provided sustenance for the Vanimo, canoe making was a family endeavor and integral to communal survival and prosperity.

Finsch also travelled to the islands that surround the New Guinea mainland in his quest for both ethnographic data and lands to claim for the new German nation. Among the objects that Finsch collected, some of the most striking are the *malangan* masks of the north coast of New Ireland, one of which is shown in **figure 11**. These masks, also known as *tatanua*, were worn by male dancers during malangan ceremonies—funerary rites designed for family members to communicate with the recently deceased. The word *malangan* generally refers to these rituals, as well as to the culture and carving style. The masks are asymmetrical in design—often incorporating coral, human hair, vegetable fiber, shells, pigments, and wood, along with motifs related to the deceased's community. This particular mask is noteworthy for the leaf-shaped patterns on the cheeks, which appear to have been made with graphite pencil. Finsch draws no attention to this feature in his notes, which could indicate that he was entirely unaware how an object like this could upset his notions of Stone Age technologies.

The Finsch Collection

The Finsch collection at the American Museum of Natural History is very much an exemplary "Stone Age" collection, gathered to preserve what was envisioned as a vanishing culture, as well as to catalogue those peoples brought into the German Empire, even if temporarily. The illustrations of the artifacts selected from the Finsch collection that appear in the following pages and in the exhibition are examples of this phenomenon. Finsch's collection was gathered from a vast regional space and is representative of diverse cultures and environments. His collection is a classic example of the Victorian idea of the "natural world," combining the material culture of pre-industrial peoples with unworked raw materials as well as the flora and fauna indigenous to these same localities. The careful notes he recorded on object cards were rarely perfunctory and display cultural insights that many of his peers lacked. Like his contemporaries, Finsch favored a technical approach to description, which is reflected in the translations that accompany the objects presented below.

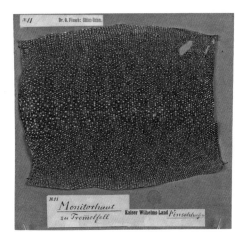

Monitor lizard skin for a drumhead

From Finsch's notes:

Locale: Finschhafen (Finsch Harbor). Region: Kaiser Wilhelmsland (German New Guinea). Monitor skin used to cover the barrel of a drum.

The fresh skin of a 1–1.5-meter-long lizard is frequently stretched over the barrel of a drum, with feet and nails still attached. The lizard skin used in New Pomerania is called "Palai" and is identical (as is this example) to *Varanus indicus* (*Monitor chlorostigma*).

In New Guinea the drum is the most loved instrument near and far, predominately in an hourglass form furnished with a handle. The Dudai District of British New Guinea had drums besides the usual types that are frequently distinguished by beautiful engraved ornaments on a unique, custom-manufactured drum.

Fig. 4 Monitor lizard skin for a drumhead. Finschhafen, Madang Province, Papua New Guinea, late 19th century. Monitor lizard skin; cardboard, ink on paper. Courtesy of the Division of Anthropology, American Museum of Natural History, ST/ 648 (Cat. 2).

Headrest

From Finsch's notes:

Locale: Finschhafen (Finsch Harbor).
Region: Kaiser Wilhelmsland
(German New Guinea).
Headrest, finely pierced carving in
hardwood.

A very old, well-formed piece, with beautiful
ornamentation that differs on both sides. The
deeply engraved patterns were undoubtedly
rubbed with chalk. Between the 13 headrests
I collected at Finsch Harbor, none were alike in
either form or ornamentation.

Fig. 5 Headrest. Finschhafen, Madang Province, Papua New Guinea, late 19th century.
Wood, traces of pigment or dirt. Courtesy of the Division of Anthropology, American Museum
of Natural History, ST/1090 (Cat. 12).

Feathers

From Finsch's notes:

Locale: New Guinea, Astrolabe Mountains.
Region: Melanesia.
Feather samples from eclectus parrots, *Eclectus polychlorus* (Scop.).

(a) 1 wing feather from a green male with an attached
    back feather.
(b) 1 of the same from a male.
(c) 1 tail feather from a male.
(d) 1 tail feather with a yellow cockatoo crest feather
    and a tail feather from a *Trichoglossus massena*.
(e) 1 small feather from a male with attached (red)
    lory feather.
(f) 2 feathers (from tail and wing) of a red female.

This bird species—spread throughout New Guinea, the Bismarck Archipelago, and neighboring islands—is one of the most common and is especially noteworthy because of its striking gender differences, which are well known among the natives. The male is colored green; the female is colored red and was therefore earlier characterized as an individual type (*E. linnei* Wagl). Because these feathers are enjoyed everywhere as ornaments, especially those of the red female, this parrot species is often kept alive.

Typically, feathers from this type of parrot are used together with others, and next to the cockatoos they form the majority of feather material. The Koiari like to use these feathers to decorate stone clubs; in Kaiser Wilhelm Country one creates headdresses from these feathers or decorates cleaning combs with them. On Hammacherfluss I saw the dried head of this parrot used as a headdress, just as those in Tagai'i were decorated with such heads.

In New Pomerania, the feathers of these Oceanic eclectus parrots ("Kalanger") still exist and are used as ornaments for headdresses and spears.

Fig. 6 Feathers. Astrolabe Mountains, Papua New Guinea, late 19th century. Eclectus parrot feathers; cardboard, ink on paper, string, copper alloy. Courtesy of the Division of Anthropology, American Museum of Natural History, ST/1945 A–F (Cat. 16).

Red loam sample

From Finsch's notes:

Locale: New Guinea, Port Moresby.
Region: Melanesia.
"Rario," fine sand.

These loam samples were collected in the environs of Port Moresby, where the women have gathered and thoroughly purified them—that is, beaten them with a stone into small pieces from which the small pieces are selected. A trough made from a broken piece of canoe serves as a base. The three loam types were ordinarily consolidated in the same amounts. Red loam is almost only used for baskets. The gritty loam bulk mixed with water is abundant, kneaded with fine sand in its final step of processing.

Fig. 7 Red loam sample. Motu culture, Port Moresby, Papua New Guinea, late 19th century. Glass, loam; metal wire, thread, ink on paper. Courtesy of the Division of Anthropology, American Museum of Natural History, ST/1052 (Cat. 8).

Bilum

From Finsch's notes:

Locale: New Guinea, Port Moresby. Region: Melanesia. Carrying sack for men.

"Waiina"; 4⅜ inches long; less than 13⅜ inches wide, thus small, thin, and long; made from dark cord, finely meshed; front has a natural (dirty) cord ground woven with pretty Greek patterns in black; the upper narrow edge is a tubular knit.

Fig. 8 *Bilum* (pack net). Motu culture, Port Moresby, Papua New Guinea, late 19th century. Plant fiber thread, dye; ink on paper. Courtesy of the Division of Anthropology, American Museum of Natural History, ST/1385 (Cat. 13).

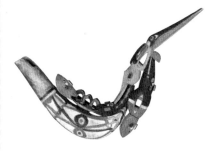
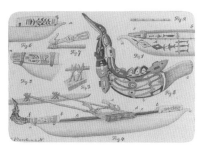

Canoe head carving and Canoe with prow

From Finsch's notes:

Locale: German New Guinea or Kaiser Wilhelmsland, Vanimo; Angriffshafen (Attack Harbor), Finsch Coast.
Region: Melanesia.
Canoe beak; artful woodcarving, colorfully painted.
Original object pictured in "Vehicles," pl. 23 (83), fig. 8, p. 141.

The piece would attach at its base notch to the bow of a canoe. Only a very few canoes display such ornaments and rarely on both ends.

These ornaments belong to the original and best work of the Papuan arts and are further distinguished by the use of a wide array of colors, some of which lie outside the usual palette of red, white, and black (for instance, yellow ochre). Some pieces have openwork, others relief work—always consisting of fantastical fish figures, which is the prevailing motif. The top usually terminates in a bird's head. However, each individual piece varies in its detail.

The similar art of canoe decoration is also found in Sechstrohfluss and Humboldt Bay, though with different detailing.

Fig. 9 Canoe head carving. Vanimo culture, Angriffshafen, Papua New Guinea, late 19th century. Wood, pigment. Courtesy of the Division of Anthropology, American Museum of Natural History, ST/1093 (Cat. 17).

Fig. 10 Otto Finsch. Canoe with prow, late 19th century. Watercolor. Papers of Otto Finsch, accession file 1898-49, box 55, plate 23. Courtesy of the Division of Anthropology, American Museum of Natural History.

Tatanua

From Finsch's notes:

Locale: Nusa Island, New
Mecklenburg, New Ireland.
Region: Bismarck Archipelago.
Mask for dancing, modeled after
the head of a native;
very fine piece.

This type of finely painted headpiece, with sublimely
carved, openwork ears, is rarely found with identical
decoration on either side of its crest. The left side of
the head has a white ground with an oblong central
field in red, outlined in blue kernels (*Abrus?*). The
remaining surface is covered in wooden spikes. The
right side is black and covered in strings of coconut
twine, with a Raupenhelm-like* central diving crest
of yellow-colored banana leaves.

*Finsch is almost certainly simply observing what
the crest reminds him of rather than declaring that
the design was inspired by the distinctive Bavarian
helmets of the Napoleonic era. Nevertheless, this
does stand as a good example of a collector's
perceiving things in terms of what he already
understands and knows.

Fig. 11 *Tatanua* (mask for funerary ceremony). Malagan culture, New Ireland, Nusa Island,
Papua New Guinea, late 19th century. Wood, shell, pigment, plant fiber, seed, resin, bark
cloth, paper. Courtesy of the Division of Anthropology, American Museum of Natural History,
ST/ 691 (Cat. 3).

Skate skin used as a spear sheath

From Finsch's notes:

Locale: Gilbert Islands (Kiribati), Tarawa.
Region: Micronesia.
Skate skin for sheathing a spear.

This prickly skate* skin is frequently the basis of a top-notch spear covering.

*The skate is a fish belonging to the Rajidae family.

Fig. 12 Skate skin used as a spear sheath. I-Kiribati culture, Tarawa, Kiribati, late 19th century. Skate skin. Courtesy of the Division of Anthropology, American Museum of Natural History, ST/ 758 AB (Cat. 5).

Hand club

From Finsch's notes:

Locale: Massim area.
Region: Papua New Guinea.
Ebony hand club, sword-shaped,
with artfully engraved pattern.
Original in Otto Finsch,
*Ethnologischer Atlas: Typen
aus der Steinzeit Neu-Guineas*
(Leipzig: Ferdinand Hirt, 1888),
p. 11, figs. 4 and 5.

The intaglio pattern is rubbed with chalk and thus
stands out quite effectively. The holes at the striking
end are used to attach tiny red shell tubes and
similar items as ornamentation. Oftentimes hair ties
and small eggshells adorn the grip. I also obtained
clubs of this sort from Maralan (Fergusson Island)
and from Kiriwina (Trobriand).

Fig. 13 Hand club. Massim, Papua New Guinea, late 19th century. Wood, pigment. Courtesy
of the Division of Anthropology, American Museum of Natural History, ST/ 850 (Cat. 7).

Boomerang

From Finsch's notes:

Locale: Queensland.
Region: Australia.
Wooden boomerang, flat, lightly
bent with some engravings.

This is a weak, curved boomerang—though not the
returning kind—and is slightly curved to the right of
center. Natives of Cape York Peninsula are the only
Australians who have no knowledge of boomerangs.

Fig. 14 Boomerang. Queensland, Australia, late 19th century. Wood, pigment. Courtesy of
the Division of Anthropology, American Museum of Natural History, ST/ 764 (Cat. 6).

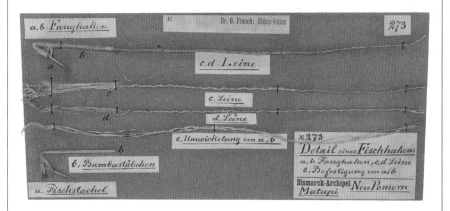

Fishhooks (*Aibo*)

From Finsch's notes:
Locale: New Britain,
Matupi Island.
Region: Melanesia.
Fishhook with line and a
demonstration of its composition.

Fishhook (a) is made of a fish spine (Ageo), to which (b), the bent end of a bamboo stalk, is attached by means of (c) and (d), which are made of two strands of twisted fiber (Lakwa) line, which with (e) a fibrous material of Lakwa in the length of the bamboo stalk and base of the hook wrap around said stalk and hook (a) and (b).

Fig. 15 Fishhooks (*Aibo*). Matupi culture, Matupi Island, New Britain, Papua New Guinea, late 19th century. Plant fiber, fish spine; cardboard, copper alloy, ink on paper. Courtesy of the Division of Anthropology, American Museum of Natural History, ST/ 946 (Cat. 10).

Water vessel

From Finsch's notes:

Locale: Admiralty Islands, Papua New Guinea.
Region: Melanesia.
Water vessel from a coconut shell, very artfully woven.

This ground coconut (of approx. 1½ pints volume) has a long, attenuated shape. Like so much of native work here, the delicate wickerwork (worked from coconut fibers) that supports the coconut—a midband ⅛ inch wide graduating into nineteen narrow strings—is exceptionally crafted.

Fig. 16 Water vessel. Admiralty Islands, Papua New Guinea, late 19th century. Coconut shell, plant fiber thread, dye. Courtesy of the Division of Anthropology, American Museum of Natural History, ST/1025 (Cat. 11).

Axe with handle

From Finsch's notes:

Locale: New Guinea, Kaile.
Region: Melanesia.
Stone blade and axe with handle.

Stone axe; black type, very wide and thick and finely chiseled blade, protruding 4¾ inches and affixed with a band 4¾ inches wide of split and finely woven rattan. The thick wooden handle, once longer, has been shortened through damage.

Fig. 17 Axe with handle. Kaile, Papua New Guinea, late 19th century. Stone, wood, plant fiber thread. Courtesy of the Division of Anthropology, American Museum of Natural History, ST/1133 A-E (Cat. 14).

Notes

1   Deniker, *The Races of Man*.

2   Ibid., 475–476.

3   Ibid., 475.

4   Scott, *A Short History of Australia*, 185. The book was used as an instructive text at the Armidale Teachers' College in New South Wales.

5   Ibid., 185–186.

6   Henry Ling Roth, "On the Use and Display of Anthropological Collections in Museums," 288.

7   Tylor, *Primitive Culture*, 21.

8   See Daniel and Renfrew, *The Idea of Prehistory*, 38–39.

9   Ibid., 46.

10   Griffiths, *Hunters and Collectors*, 19–20.

11   Anonymous, "Geography and Travels," 189.

12   Howes, "'It Is Not So!'" and *Germanica Pacifica*.

13   The group was actually a conglomerate of three other groups formed or funded by the entrepreneur Adolph von Hansemann: the Sea Trade Society, the New Guinea Consortium, and the Astrolabe Bay Company. For the sake of brevity, I use the informal designation "South Sea Plotters."

14   See Hempenstall, *Pacific Islanders under German Rule*, 16–17.

15   Ibid., 163.

16   Ibid., 164.

17   Ibid., 165.

18   For a detailed discussion of Finsch's career disappointments, see the conclusion of Howes's *Germanica Pacifica*.

19   Rainer Buschmann describes Finsch's collection as "valuable and groundbreaking." Buschmann, *Anthropology's Global Histories*, 37.

20   Ibid., 6.

21   Penny, *Objects of Culture*, 79.

22   Ibid.

23   Finsch to Putnam, December 1896, Papers of Otto Finsch, accession file 1898-49, Division of Anthropology, AMNH.

24   Finsch, *Ethnologischer Atlas*.

25   Finsch to Putnam, February 1896, Papers of Otto Finsch, accession file 1898-49, Division of Anthropology, AMNH.

26   Howes, *Germanica Pacifica*, 276.

27   Boas to Jesup, July 1898, Papers of Otto Finsch, accession file 1898-49, Division of Anthropology, AMNH.

28   Osborn, *History, Plan and Scope of the American Museum of Natural History*, 107.

29   The translations of Finsch's notes are by Erin Alexa Freedman and Lara Schilling. I have adapted the translations for a general audience, while preserving Finsch's often dry prose and his meaning.

30   The full details of this analysis will be available in Rowlands and Jarillo de la Torre, "Not by Blood, but Some Iron."

31   The Peabody collection was mostly acquired before, during, or only a few decades after Finsch ventured into the Pacific. The rate of cross-cultural entanglement in the Peabody collection stands at roughly 18 percent and may be revised upward after I revisit pigmentation sampling to determine whether the material is indigenous or foreign.

Two
"All Is Race"
Anthropology and
Colonial Control

In Benjamin Disraeli's novel *Tancred* (1847), the character Sidonia says: "All is race; there is no other truth."[1] Not simply the idle musing of a fictional character, this is a reflection of Disraeli's own view on the nature of civilization. Five years later, Disraeli repeats the idea: "Progress and reaction are but words to justify the millions. They mean nothing, they are nothing, they are phrases and not facts. All is race. In the structure, the decay, and the development of the various families of man, the vicissitudes of history will find their main solution."[2] Race theory had steadily begun to replace religion as the main justification for the exploitation of foreign peoples in the industrial age. This chapter explores ideas of racial purity, adventure travel, imperial power, and levels of civilization. In a discussion of the intersection of race theory, government authority, and colonial collecting in Oceania, two government agents in Queensland in the 1890s through 1905 merit particular attention. Contemporaries and rivals, Walter Edmund Roth (1861–1933) and Archibald Meston (1851–1924) both saw themselves as experts on the state's Aboriginal population. Roth was a prolific collector (his objects are not featured in the exhibition) who authored many scholarly volumes on the Aboriginal people of Queensland. Fellow government agent Meston very much fits the mold of the imperial adventurer. Both men were very sympathetic to Aboriginal people and drew the ire of business and political opponents who objected to government interference in the exploitation of indigenous lives and labor. The chapter closes with a discussion of John William Waters's collection from Fiji, which contains notable examples of material adaptation at odds with the prevailing narrative of purity in race and in objects, thus further demonstrating the entanglement of race, politics, and collecting.

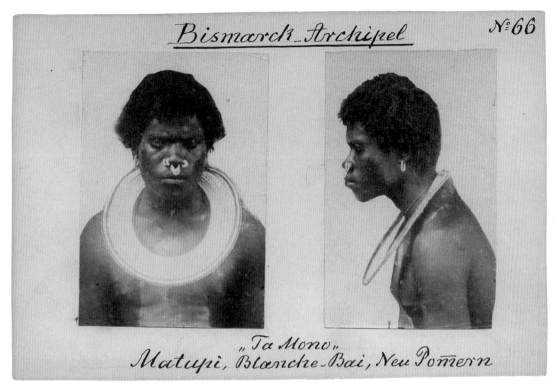

Fig. 18 Otto Finsch. "Ta Mono," from Matupi Island, Blanche Bay, New Pomern, 1884–85. Papers of Otto Finsch, accession file 1898-49. Courtesy of the Division of Anthropology, American Museum of Natural History.

Race Theory and Social Hierarchies

For many scientists of the post-Enlightenment period, the fundamental difference between people of the world was beyond question. John Pinkerton, in his *Dissertation on the Origin of the Scythians or Goths* (1787), stated that "a Tartar, a Negro, an American & c. & c. differ as much from a German, as a bull-dog, or lap-dog, or shepherd's cur, from a pointer."[3] As we have seen in the preceding chapter, Finsch rejected these assertions. Perhaps to his credit, Finsch conducted his fieldwork of cataloguing human beings by measuring them and taking comparative photographs such as the anthropometric image of "Ta Mono" **(fig. 18)**. It is indicative of his impartiality that the conclusions he drew from this kind of photography are not the same as those of the majority of his peers. Along with fellow Germans Adolf Meyer and Felix von Luschan, he was one of a small number of emerging scholars who dismissed race theory or pointed to its inherent flaws.

Johann Friedrich Blumenbach (1752–1840), one of the most influential theorists on the classification of racial types, had argued that race theory should not be used as a means to deny human affinity. Although he had mostly followed the racial classifications of Carolus Linnaeus, Blumenbach changed Linnaeus's four-race model of humanity to a five-race model. He saw the divisions as being dictated by geography, skin color, temperament, and posture.[4] Of these, geography was the most significant, as Blumenbach asserted that racial variations would change if members of a race were to inhabit a different environment or were subjected to a markedly different climate.[5] Unlike many of the scientists who accepted his classificatory system, Blumenbach rejected the ·notion that races were inherently different from one another. He wrote that "although there seems to be so great a difference between widely separate nations, that you might easily take the inhabitants of the Cape of Good Hope, the Greenlanders, and the Circassians for so many different species of man, yet when the matter is thoroughly considered, you see that all do so run into one another, and that one variety of mankind does so sensibly pass into the other, that you cannot mark out the limits between them."[6]

Despite Blumenbach's claims for the universality of humankind, nineteenth-century race theory is primarily an ideology of dominance. Race theory in the Victorian era was inherently antagonistic and served to justify the subjugation of others. In *English Traits* (1856), Ralph Waldo Emerson observes that "it is race, is it not? that puts the hundred millions of India under the dominion of a remote island in the north of Europe."[7] Even before the publication of Charles Darwin's *On the Origin of Species* (1859), racial theorists stressed that the extinction of presumed lesser races was inevitable. In his *Races of Men* (1850), the controversial Robert Knox observes that because the dark-skinned races are "destined by the nature of their race to run, like all other animals, a certain limited course of existence, it matters little how their extinction is brought about."[8] Knox believed that Anglo-Saxons were the preeminent "race," a belief not without its irony, given that Knox, a Scot, was of Celtic, not Anglo-Saxon ancestry.

Social Darwinism and its adherents viewed the human race as belonging to a hierarchy, commonly referred to as the Great Chain of Being. Although the concept is from the Renaissance, Social Darwinism divorces the Great Chain of Being from its purely religious context and applies it to a hierarchy in which human beings are placed according to their position of power. The European instigators of the theory naturally saw themselves at the top. Race theory, combined with new scientific research, appeared to justify domination.[9] If authority and servitude were states of being, then European domination over those considered to be on a lower scale of civilization was a matter dictated by nature. Thus, in the case of Australia, Aboriginal people were placed at the very bottom of the racial hierarchy.[10] The chief interest for the European observer was how a study of "primitive" people could contribute to knowledge about the "higher races" and what they could tell anthropology and history about the prehistory of Europe.[11] As the century progressed, innovations in publishing, particularly from 1870 onward, meant that pamphlets and articles perpetuating the idea of racial hierarchy could be widely disseminated.[12]

Race theory was not exclusive to Great Britain or continental Europe. The United States had also begun to pioneer in this regard. The seemingly unchallenged imperial triumph of both the United States and Britain had contributed to the study of what was perceived as a shared Anglo-Saxon racial dominance.[13] In the United States, science was conscripted to justify the string of conquests over Native American people and territory and the exploitation of African lives and labor. Colonial experience contributed to the growth of race theory because of the need of the powerful to find moral justification for subjugation and exploitation. In the territories of the European, British, and American empires (among which Oceania was divided), race theory was integral to the implementation of colonial policies and the exploitation and displacement of native peoples.

The idea of race is problematic because it is, as Douglas Lorimer notes, more of a mental construction than a biological one.[14] Victorian-era scientists were often frustrated by the imprecise and colloquial use of the term "race." But it is precisely because the term is so difficult to define that it became an axiomatic construct and almost impossible to discredit. The essays in *Foreign Bodies: Oceania and the Science of Race, 1750–1940* (2010) explore this essentially unstable theorization of race in depth, analyzing the "tensions, inconsistencies, and instability of rival discourses" of race theory with a focus on the "intersections of metropolitan biology or anthropology and encounters in the field."[15] In a similar fashion, *Darwin's Laboratory* (1994) examines the ways in which the Pacific served as a testing ground for nineteenth-century evolutionary theories and the relation of the theories to constructions and treatment of peoples.[16] According to most modern studies of the subject, ethnographic collection and imperial triumphalism are linked predominantly by conceptions of race. Race was a means by which Europeans endeavored to explain their triumphs. It was just one means of doing so, although it seems unlikely that an absence of race theory would have meant an absence of colonialism. Darwin's *On the Origin of Species* is usually regarded as the greatest influence on conceptions of racial hierarchy; for instance, the second chapter of Stephen J. Gould's exposé of the sciences of craniometry, phrenology, and other forms of intellectual measurement is titled "Before Darwin," as if everything that happened subsequently is a consequence of Darwin's theory of evolution.[17]

Although racism and hierarchies of being are undeniably part of the Victorian scientific mind-set, an overemphasis on racial thought in studies of the period has inadvertently downplayed other cultural factors that inspired and influenced ethnographers. Rainer Buschmann observes that those who set out to explore uncharted territories and unknown peoples often did so with motivations other than imperial enterprise.[18] Some collectors only sought profit—for example, Francis Lyons, who tried to sell the skull of an Aboriginal mummy to the Queensland Museum in the late nineteenth century. Others, including Meston, probably advertised their credentials as worthy cataloguers of Aboriginal culture to gain social recognition and a government position. In an article on nineteenth-century travel writing, David Seed links casual adventurism and empire.[19] According to Seed, travelers, merely by seeing, participated in empire building because, through their interpretation of what they saw, they contributed to the "appropriations of imperialism."[20] They constructed the "other" by visually identifying what was foreign and through commentaries in their diaries and travelogues. Ethnographers, particularly amateur collectors of indigenous artifacts, behaved just like the travel writers of their day. As noted in chapter 1, collection and ethnography were forms of adventurism, a kind of sport that simultaneously manufactured identity. Against the backdrop of the adventurism and racially charged science of the day, observers shaped the identities of the familiar and the foreign.[21]

The Guard of Honor and the Sacred Ibis

On March 26, 1896, the *Brisbane Courier* reported expectantly on the official festivities planned for the arrival of the new governor of Queensland:

> At the reception of Lord Lamington there will be an innovation unknown at the welcome of any previous Governor. At the request of the Municipal Council, and with the approval of the Colonial Secretary, Mr. A. Meston will organize an aboriginal guard of honour, to consist of twenty carefully selected aboriginals, who will represent seven

different tribes, all in their various warpaints with plumes, armlets, necklaces, head bands, and spears, nullas, boomerangs, and shields. All Queensland weapons from Brisbane to the Gulf will be displayed. This will be a spectacle new even to Brisbane, and will doubtless be a specially interesting and instructive part of the programme.[22]

The display was one of the many efforts of the Scottish entrepreneur, journalist, writer, and politician Archibald Meston to advertise the character, uniqueness, and value of the state's native population, along with publicizing his own abilities. Meston, as many scholars have pointed out, was nothing if not an aggressive self-promoter, but his respect and admiration for Aboriginal people was genuine.[23] He had earned the nickname "the Sacred Ibis" during a debate on immigration because, according to Cheryl Taylor, of his "esoteric references in an extravagantly pretentious speech which he delivered as a young man to the Legislative Assembly."[24] In the early 1890s, Meston formed the "Wild Australia Show," which consisted of a troupe of Aboriginals and Torres Strait Islanders that toured Sydney and Melbourne and had ambitious plans to travel abroad. But funds ran out, and Meston left his performers stranded in Melbourne for six months.[25] His planned exhibition of an "Aboriginal honor guard" before the governor came on the heels of his own government-supported studies in Queensland of the condition of the indigenous populations.

Figure 19 shows the actual event, with Meston himself visible on the extreme left of the photograph, looking toward the camera and wearing a military-style suit. The honor guard of eighteen Aboriginal men is staged on the freshly kept lawn of Government House, before dignitaries of the state that ruled them, as authentic examples of the cultures they were selected to represent. The situation is an entirely constructed one, brought about by the interactions of colonial authorities with the people they governed and the ambitions of an amateur ethnographer. The event is a good example of cultural entanglement. The press regarded it as a resounding success. The *Queenslander* printed the following account on April 25:

The aboriginal guard of honour, one of the most interesting parts of the procession at Lord Lamington's reception, and on whose entire success Mr. Meston is to be congratulated, represented widely scattered tribes and many dialects. There were Nerang Creek men who spoke "Yoocum," Ipswich men who spoke "Yuggara." Stradbroke Islandmen who spoke "Coobennpil," a Moreton Islander speaking "Gnoogee." A Bribie Islander who spoke "Nhulla," a Maranoa man speaking "Cogai," a Darling Downs man who spoke "Wacca," a Dawson River man speaking "Coonggarrie," and a Diamantina River man. They all arrived in Brisbane the day before the Governor, and were only told the same night and next morning what Mr. Meston required them to do. They stripped and painted themselves, in the yard at the Museum, and marched thence to Howard Smith's wharf, where they arrived at 2 o'clock, and were drawn up in single file to receive the Governor, whom they welcomed with a song of the old times. They marched up Queen-street at the head of the procession in perfect order in double

Fig. 19 "Aboriginal guard April, 1896." Albumen photographic print. Courtesy of the Peabody Museum of Archaeology and Ethnology, Harvard University, PM 2004.29.21641 (digital file #160400070).

file of twelve each, with the proud and stately tread characteristic of the Australian blacks in their wild state. On the following Saturday Mr. Meston received a wire of invitation from Government House, and marched eighteen of the blacks to see Lord and Lady Lamington in their new home. The Governor was very kind to the aboriginals, and greatly admired their fine physique and athletic appearance. The following are the native names of the eighteen who visited Government House:— Yangurra, Dalillie, Palowarie, Warroo, Jallanda, Yagooin, Goonjaringa, Turyan-myan, Munyan-dyan, Ningeribee, Jacoora, Nuggin, Cangando, Yeerimbam, Gootiggarie, Wamgool, Janjarrigo, Chamgoroo.[26]

That Meston would go to the trouble to communicate the individual names of the participants in the honor guard is itself quite remarkable and is a testament to his more humanitarian impulses. A complex and often contradictory figure, Meston was sympathetic to the plight of the Aboriginal people of Queensland, but he nonetheless staged this event as a classic construction of a "primitive" race. The participants were "stripped" so as to portray their "wild state." When the new governor asked "whether something could be done to preserve the race from extinction," Meston explained his own work and stated that the "Government, and especially the Colonial Secretary, were very desirous of bettering the condition of the blacks."[27] The entire incident illustrates the relation between government authority over their colonized subjects and the construction of these subjects as racial archetypes, imprisoned by their own culture in a "backward" stage of life and technology. Meston's commitment to Aboriginal health, evident in his government survey work, and his staged political maneuvering of the Aborginal people as "interesting and instructive" set-piece exhibits for powerful individuals certainly secured his own future in the colonial administration of Aboriginal affairs for a while, but he was eventually superseded by the learned and highly respected ethnographer Walter Edmund Roth.

Roth was a colonial administrator, an avid collector of material culture, and a direct observer and commentator on the Aboriginal people of Queensland. Born into a family that gained renown in the fields of ethnology and anthropology, he was the son of Mathias Roth—a Hungarian Jew who had resettled in Britain— and the younger brother of the anthropologist Henry Ling Roth, most noted for *The Aborigines of Tasmania* (1890), a compilation of all the sources he could find on the Aboriginal people of Tasmania (then thought to be extinct).[28] Roth graduated from Oxford with honors in biology and traveled to Australia twice, punctuating these stays with his studies in medicine in Britain. Roth first worked in Australia as a schoolmaster of boys' grammar schools in both Sydney and Brisbane and then, after qualifying as a surgeon, as a doctor in hospitals in Boulia, Cloncurry, and Normanton. His most notable roles in Australia, however, were his tenure as Protector of Aborigines in Queensland from 1897 to 1906 and his posting as a royal commissioner in Western Australia in 1904.[29]

Roth's interest in anthropology began after he finished his medical training. In 1897, he published a meticulous work titled *Ethnographical Studies among the North-West-Central Queensland Aborigines*,[30] which was soon widely distributed to policemen and mission stations on the frontier. The book was partly responsible for his being offered the post of northern Protector of Queensland Aborigines.[31] Meston, who had been instrumental in the creation of the Aboriginals Protection and Restriction of the Sale of Opium Act,[32] filled the post of Southern Protector from 1898 to 1903. In her article on Meston's journalism, Cheryl Taylor heaps praise on Roth at Meston's expense: "Neither Meston's notes and reports nor his newspaper accounts bear comparison as professional writing with Roth's patient documenting and illustrating of all aspects of tribal life, records which were subsequently published in scholarly volumes."[33] The Queensland government passed the Opium Act in 1897, ostensibly to protect Aboriginal populations from European and Chinese exploitation.[34] The legislation created an administrative body to oversee the regulation and protection of Aboriginal people, including marriage and work rights. A Chief Protector was appointed to act in concert with local protectors, police, and civil servants in implementing the legislation.[35] In 1904, the notoriously difficult and allegedly brutal Meston was removed from office, and Roth was made the overall protector of Queensland Aborigines, a post he held until his resignation in 1906.[36]

Although their tenures as protectors were relatively short-lived, the two men provide a clear example of the interrelationship of anthropology and colonial authority over native populations. Meston had no university education, and Roth never formally studied anthropology, but both were committed to the study of Australian Aboriginal people, and they both acquired substantial field experience and collections of Aboriginal material culture. In addition, Roth published multiple volumes on the Aboriginal population of Queensland. Meston and Roth provide good examples of Peter Pels's description of the role of anthropology in empire: anthropological research provides a cheap and bloodless alternative to colonial strategies of violence and extermination.[37] Research was an arm of paternalistic racism.

The researcher could provide information that aided the government in better controlling subject populations. Edward Said's *Orientalism* (1978) explores the relations between research and government, the scholar's intent and the corporate use of power. The corporate or institutional element legitimizes research by employing it as an educational tool, creating knowledge of the "other" and arbitrating this knowledge as best suits the realities of government.[38] Research, therefore, provides legitimacy to colonial policy.

As noted earlier, both Roth and Meston collected ethnological artifacts of the Aboriginal people they studied and administered. Meston's collection, housed at the Queensland Museum, is not well known, whereas Roth's collection is one of the best known, not only in Australia (with holdings at the Queensland Museum and the Australia Museum),[39] but worldwide (with holdings at the British Museum, the Smithsonian Institution, and the Walter Roth Museum in Georgetown, Guyana). This division is largely the result of Roth's own extensive travels and links to multiple institutions, as well as the inability of any one of these institutions to take his entire collection at the time. Although Roth explored the cultural dimension of the artifacts he collected in his ethnographic literature, their identification with the highly esteemed Roth Collection has the effect of distancing them from their native heritage.

Because of the positions of authority that first Meston and then Roth occupied, the scientific notions of race and purity that underpinned their intellectual study affected their governance and management of the Aboriginal people. Roth, in particular, used the powers granted in a 1901 amendment to the Opium Act to restrict marriage and reduce the "half-caste problem." The amendment was meant to make all mixed marriages with Aboriginal people subject to the discretion of the protector. Regina Ganter has persuasively argued that Roth was most interested in using such restrictions to stop Aboriginal procreation with "Asiatics."[40] This agenda is undeniably related to the ideas of distinction, hierarchy, and race that were held by scientists and anthropologists of the day. But more particularly, it shows that the agents who operated under these laws believed that "purity" of race was attainable.

During the colonial period, ideas of race permeated interpretations of and interactions with Aboriginal artifacts. Just as the value placed on purity affected discussions of race, so too did the idea of material purity affect the discussion of mixed or cross-cultural objects. In the process of capturing and cataloguing collections, especially when they are associated with government agents such as Roth, the weighted bias toward the imagined pure object—the "unentangled" artifact—could have the effect of silencing the makers' own narratives of power.

John William Waters in Fiji

The process of silencing was, of course, not restricted to Australia. Consider, for instance, the collection from Fiji of professional photographer John William Waters (1851–?) at the American Museum of Natural History, containing several instances in which the pursuit of authenticity clouds the interpretation of material and the native voice in an object. The disbursal of funds by Mrs. Morris Jesup made the collection possible, leading to the acquisition of around 1,800 specimens.[41] Waters had spent four decades living in Fiji, and his collection, according to the museum, "is especially valuable in that it represents the life of the Fijians before they had become acquainted with iron and its uses."[42] Waters had been given a hundred dollars to purchase curios in 1899, a decade before the museum acquired the collection. Franz Boas had recommended Waters to the museum director, Morris Jesup, as a collection agent who had "a very good idea of the ethnology of those islands [Fiji], and could be of great service to this Museum."[43] Given that Waters had such limited funds to work with, his collection is a remarkable achievement. His accession file fills eight typed pages, listing objects, with sketches of objects and photographs of islanders. The objects are mostly from Fiji, but other islands are represented. The object list, like most other collection records, is extensive, although contextually sparse. The most detail is given for objects that are often associated in the European imagination with "savage" and horrifying deeds, such as object number 70: "1 Cannibal fork . . . Used by chiefs in partaking of human cooked flesh considered a delicacy."

The very first objects listed in the accession file are "3 Very old fighting breastplates." No further detail is given, although the accession records come with a page of sketches drawn, judging by the notation at the bottom right, by an A. G. Macgregor in 1908. At the bottom left, two of the breastplates are depicted, described merely as "ornamental" **(fig. 20)**. The process of cataloguing these pieces in this way has had the effect of removing them from their historical and cultural context. The two objects **(fig. 21)** are not mere ornaments but *civatabua* (or *civavonovono*)—highly prized objects often made from whale ivory and pearl shell. Intended for Fijian chiefs, the breastplates were fashioned by Tongan and Samoan canoe builders. According

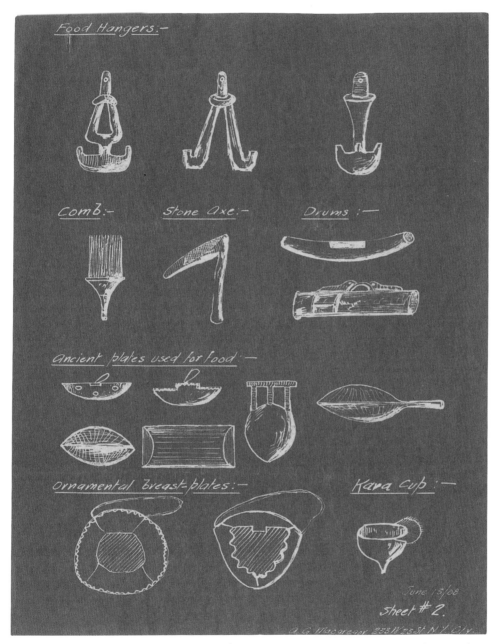

Fig. 20 A.G. Macgregor. Sketches of objects from the John William Waters Archive, June 13, 1908. Courtesy of the Division of Anthropology, American Museum of Natural History.

Fig. 21 *Civitabua*, or *civavonovono* (breastplates). Fiji, late 19th century. Pearl oyster shell, sperm whale tooth, white metal, plant fiber. (*left*) Courtesy of the Division of Anthropology, American Museum of Natural History, 80.0/2061 (Cat. 27); (*right*) Courtesy of the Division of Anthropology, American Museum of Natural History, 80.0/2062 (Cat. 28).

to Anita Herle and Lucie Carreau, the civatabua were constructed in such a way that their structural integrity remained invisible.[44] The stitching that binds the pieces together, employing the same craft as canoe building, can be seen only from the back. The invisible binding likely contributed to the belief that the artifacts held magical power. The breastplates were, in fact, thought to confer supernatural invulnerability in battle. No doubt they did provide protection from long-range Fijian arrows, although they were probably mainly status and prestige pieces.

To manufacture these objects, the maker would grind down several whale's teeth into thin, relatively flat pieces, which were then often polished and rubbed with coconut oil. The oil would have the effect of darkening the material, as is evident in **fig. 21** (*left*). The Museum's conservation team has determined that the oily brown coloration was most likely acquired through ordinary handling and wear rather than from the maker's conscious effort to color the breastplates. The construction of the very visible bindings on the front face of the breastplates is noteworthy. Multiple iron nails that have been reduced by grinding are used to hold the segments of pearl shell and whale tooth together. During the later nineteenth century, when contact with Europeans had intensified, access to metal was more widespread, although not yet commonplace. The material would have enhanced the object's prestige, although it was not the metal itself that was prestigious; rather, it provided evidence of the chief's access to and good relations with foreign traders, who were themselves representatives of powerful people. Therefore, the metal binding does not render these breastplates less inventive than breastplates that did not use iron; the association with foreign materials, however, heightens their status and that of their wearer. Contradicting Osborn's report for the Museum's trustees, which claims that the Waters collection is important because it shows the life of Fijians before iron, the breastplates demonstrate how collectors could consciously or otherwise attempt to wrest power away from those from whom they collected. The objects' complex stories serve as tangible symbols of power in their own right and bring us to the topic of adaptation.

Influenced by race theories of the day, the collections amassed by men such as Roth, Meston, and Waters are inextricably linked to the idea that technological sophistication indicates equal racial sophistication or complexity and that, consequently, the "purer" and less sophisticated technologies were the hallmarks of "lower," even retrograde races. Within the same theoretical context, the objects discussed in the next chapter highlight the presence of material adaptation in the collection record and the ways in which collectors interpreted—or ignored—these entangled objects. The material facts of an object's construction were not subject to objective recording but were instead perceived as examples of the connection between race and technology.

Notes

1   Disraeli, often-times British prime minister during the nineteenth century, was fervently pro-empire. In his *Tancred*, the character Sidonia is discussing the basis of progress and civilization.

2   Cited in Horsman, "Origins of Racial Anglo-Saxonism in Great Britain before 1850," 404.

3   Cited in ibid., 391.

4   Gould, *The Mismeasure of Man*, 403–404.

5   Ibid., 408.

6   Cited in ibid., 407.

7   Cited in Castillo, "The Best of Nations?," 108.

8   Knox, *The Races of Men*, 224. Knox was chiefly controversial because he had been involved in the Burke and Hare scandal in Edinburgh in the 1830s. According to Knox, he had unknowingly purchased the corpses of Burke and Hare's murder victims for use

in his anatomy classes. Although Knox had escaped prosecution, he was no longer able to practice anatomy. Among the many publications on this scandal, see Richardson, *Death, Dissection and the Destitute*.

9 See Griffiths, *Hunters and Collectors*, 10.

10 See Stocking, *Race, Culture, and Evolution*, 33.

11 There is also a vast amount of literature on this subject, specifically relating to how Australia was a testing ground for racial and evolutionary theories, see Frame, *Evolution in the Antipodes*; Butcher, "Darwinism, Social Darwinism, and the Australian Aborigines."

12 See Lorimer, "Race, Science and Culture," 14.

13 See Horsman, "Origins of Racial Anglo-Saxonism in Great Britain before 1850," 390.

14 See Lorimer, "Race, Science and Culture," 24.

15 Douglas and Ballard, *Foreign Bodies*, 6.

16 Macleod and Rehbock, *Darwin's Laboratory*.

17 Gould, *The Mismeasure of Man*, chap. 2.

18 Buschmann, "Uncertain Currents." For a discussion of profit seekers in the Pacific, see Igler, "Exploring the Concept of Empire in Pacific History."

19 Seed, "Nineteenth-Century Travel Writing." For more on Lyons, see: Letter from Francis Lyons, 12 January 1882, Queensland Museum Inwards Correspondence Archive 78/1882.

20 Ibid., 1.

21 Of the ample literature linking the observer's gaze to the operation of imperialism, the best known are Spurr, *The Rhetoric of Empire*, and Said, *Orientalism*.

22 "Aboriginal Guard of Honour," *Brisbane Courier*, March 26, 1896.

23 For an engaging discussion of Meston's quirks of character and ambitions, see Taylor, "Constructing Aboriginality."

24 Ibid., 124.

25 The "Wild Australia Show" was the subject of a 2015 exhibition at the University of Queensland's Anthropology Museum. See also Casey, "Colonisation, Notions of Authenticity and Aboriginal Australian Performance," 6.

26 "The Governor's Aboriginal Guard," *Queenslander*, April 25, 1896.

27 "Aboriginal Exhibition—at Government House," *Darling Downs Gazette*, April 15, 1896.

28 Henry Ling Roth, *The Aborigines of Tasmania*.

29 "Protector of Aborigines" was the official title for agents employed to oversee the administration and protection of Aboriginal people. There were various ranks in the Protection Board, but the chief protector was most commonly referred to as "the protector."

30 Walter Edmund Roth, *Ethnological Studies among the North-West-Central Queensland Aborigines*.

31 The other reason for Roth's securing the post, which the police commissioner regarded as equally important, was that he was a trained surgeon and could thus provide medical care to the people he administered.

32 For Meston's report, which led to some of the policies of the act, see Meston, *Report on the Aboriginals of Queensland*.

33 See Taylor, "Constructing Aboriginality," 124.

34 See Ganter, "WE Roth on Asians in Australia," 157–158.

35 Ibid., 158.

36 Cheryl Taylor discusses some of the discomfort Meston's sometimes harsh treatment of Aboriginal people caused among the powerful. According to Taylor's research, Meston punished infractions by chaining Aboriginal people to trees overnight or having them beaten. See Taylor, "Constructing Aboriginality," 122. See also Khan, *Catalogue of the Roth Collection*, 10; Ganter, "WE Roth on Asians in Australia," 161, 165–168; Ganter and Kidd, "The Power of Protectors."

37 Pels, "The Anthropology of Colonialism," 164.

38 Said, *Orientalism*, 2–3.

39 The Roth collection, as archaeologist Leon Satterthwait observes, is "often taken as a reference point for Australian museum collections . . . because of its size, the relatively early date at which it was collected, the extent to which it was documented, and the fact that it was compiled by a single individual and thus has a known history and a degree of coherence as a collection" (cited in Reynolds, "Australian Material Culture," 15). The collection was gathered during Roth's stay in Australia, both in his official capacity as protector and as a private citizen interested in ethnography.

40 Ganter, "WE Roth on Asians in Australia."

41 See Osborn, History; Plan and Scope of the American Museum of Natural histlry, 107.

42 Ibid.

43 Boas to Jesup, January 14, 1899, John William Waters Archive, accession file 1909-1, Division of Anthropology, AMNH.

44 Herle and Carreau, *Chiefs and Governors*, 91–92; see also Neich and Pereira, *Pacific Jewelry and Adornment*, 144–145.

Three
"Doubtful Things"
Dismissing Cultural
Entanglements

The John William Waters Archive at the American Museum of Natural History includes a photograph of an unidentified family, objectified into ethnological specimens by their anonymity and their inclusion in the archive **(fig. 22)**. Despite the absence of notes to explain when and where the image was taken, it is clearly not a photographer's attempt to render individuals into the usual anthropometric data or to dismiss their appearance. Waters operated in Fiji and was a photographer, so it is likely that he captured the image himself while working in the islands. Although this kind of image collection was relatively commonplace, photographers preferred to manufacture images that presented informative or idealized versions of the indigenous other, such as Finsch's photograph of three Motuan women from New Guinea **(fig. 23)**. Finsch's photograph presents three women dressed in grass skirts, with their upper bodies naked. Two of them appear distinctly bored or possibly hostile as they hold an enormous stitched leaf or bark barrel, while the other, seated, appears to smile. Although the camera has interrupted them, the image creates an impression that they have merely paused for a moment while going about the "gathering" of a hunter-gatherer lifestyle. Many of Finsch's photographs provide their subjects' names, unlike those of other collectors, but in this case there is no such information. The photograph records a generic slice of life—a manufactured, frozen moment of cultural activity. The subdued smile and disinterested looks of the people in the photographs should perhaps not be overanalyzed. The limits of technology at the time meant that camera subjects had to pose completely still for long periods. In fact, figure 22 is very much a classic Victorian family photograph—stoic expressions were a mainstay of portraiture, contributing to the popular conception that Europeans of the 1800s

Fig. 22 Family portrait, 1880s. John William Waters Archives. Courtesy of the Division of Anthropology, American Museum of Natural History.

Fig. 23 "Motufrauen" (Motuan women), 1884–1885. Papers of Otto Finsch, accession file 1898-49. Courtesy of the Division of Anthropology, American Museum of Natural History.

were horribly stuffy. But, of course, this family is not European, even though they wear tailored clothes, accessories, and hairstyles associated with late nineteenth-century Western fashion (note particularly their shoes and the tight ringlets of two of the children).

Waters was a commercial photographer, so it is likely that the family in this image paid for his services, which, if so, subverts the notion that European photographs of native people are mere exercises in control, cataloguing, and curiosity. Anthropologist and photographic historian Michael Aird finds that with rising affluence, Australian Aboriginal people began to purchase their own cameras or pay professionals to photograph them.[1] Although such photographs may have been conscious images of conformity with power elites and expressions of affluence, they were not always attempts at imitation—European clothing, for instance, had become commonplace for many colonized peoples.[2] For the purpose of themes of entanglement and collectors' construction of narratives, Waters's image and others like it not only demonstrate cross-cultural contact through the camera lens and the material photograph; they also subvert the idea that the people of late nineteenth- and early twentieth-century Oceania chiefly were examples of a prehistorical mode of life, frozen in time.

The photographs and objects likely had very different meanings for those who appeared in them or created them. The Waters photograph might be an expression of individual affluence, or it might be the family patriarch's conscious expression of conformity, demonstrating that he belonged to a powerful and influential group. Alternatively, the individuals captured in the frame may have been deliberately thumbing their noses at either their own society or their imperial overseers. The photograph may in fact be a form of resistance, what James C. Scott terms a "hidden transcript," in which subordinates subvert dominant power groups through a process of communication and reaction to the "public transcript."[3] Thus, the image could be considered a symbolic inversion of the relation between Europeans and Fijians. The collection record, however, lacks a full context for the image, so further speculation would be purely hypothetical.

The image of indigeneity that nineteenth- and early twentieth-century scientists constructed was nothing more than ideological conjecture. The idea that people could be stagnant and unable to adapt suited the needs of colonial government and underpinned narratives of power and exploitation. These narratives relied in part on connecting a system of classification with the material culture of those they were labeling as "prehistoric." Meston provides a clear example of the interrelation of classification, collecting, and colonial authority in his characterization of the inadaptability of those he administered. The boomerang's lack of technological development was proof, he argued, that Aboriginal people were "one of the most bigotedly conservative races of mankind."[4] At the same time that such narratives were being put forward, the scientific and political community was arguing that many of the native peoples of the world were doomed to extinction. This belief was itself ideologically determined, unsupported by any substantial research into changing populations. Historian Russell McGregor terms this belief an "axiomatic fact": everybody knew that Aboriginal people would soon be extinct, even though no one who proclaimed it was relying on anything beyond casual observation and conjecture.[5]

McGregor's research deals primarily with Queensland during the half century in which Roth and Meston were government agents employed to watch over a supposedly vanishing people. Contact with European settlers and native police on the frontier had, in fact, severely depleted the Queensland Aboriginal population. With the discovery of gold in northern Queensland, tens of thousands of Europeans and Chinese migrated to the region, eager to exploit the newfound wealth.[6] Competition with Aboriginal people for land and resources was the immediate result; the depopulation of the Aboriginal community was the ultimate consequence. Where Europeans settled, the native fauna was depleted and the wilderness cleared to make way for farmlands and communities.[7] When Aboriginal people lost access to their game and resources and hunted European livestock to compensate, settler retaliation was swift and merciless. Elsewhere in Australia, Roth's old university acquaintance and fellow ethnographer Baldwin Spencer (1860–1929) observed this pattern in the regions that he and Francis James Gillen (1855–1912) studied and decried how grossly unequal white and black relations had become.[8]

Ethnographers and anthropologists often observed the barbarities that European civilization inflicted on Aboriginal people on the Australian frontier. The rapid depopulation of Aboriginal people was certainly not limited to Queensland. In 1880, when Lorimer Fison and A. W. Howitt published their study of the Kamilaroi of northern New South Wales and the Kurnai of Gippsland, it was clear that Aboriginal populations had been profoundly depleted.[9] Howitt discusses frontier mortality in his introduction to the section on the Kurnai. According to his figures, Gippsland had an Aboriginal population of 1,000–1,500 in 1839. By 1877, a royal commission had established that the population had shrunk to 52 men, 41 women, and 66 children.[10] The population decline, according to Howitt, was the result of the contest of races on the frontier:

> It is only in accordance with previous experience as to the fate of this aboriginal race when brought into contact with the white men throughout Australia, and it is only a further instance of a general experience of that which is going on all over the world, with greater or less rapidity, under similar contact of savage coloured races with the civilized white race. . . . It may be stated broadly that the advance of settlement has, upon the frontier at least, been marked by a line of blood. . . . But the tide of settlement has advanced along an ever-widening line, breaking the native tribes with its first waves and overwhelming their wrecks with its flood.[11]

Combined with an analysis of material culture as material stagnation, such claims convinced the European imagination that native extinction was inevitable. Thus, W. L. Cleland, president of the Royal Society of South Australia, argued in his 1899 address to the society that the "non-plasticity . . . of the [Aboriginal] race as a whole" meant that it could not survive long in the modern world.[12]

Of course, the populations that the theorists insisted could not survive have done so. European collectors' fetishization of so-called pure or authentic examples of native culture blinded them to the evidence that was readily apparent in the objects they acquired. Although adaptation, not stagnation, was commonplace, collectors who acknowledged adaptation wrote it off as either degeneration or assimilation to the imperial culture, as Waters may have done with the family he photographed. When objects were viewed favorably, as authentic, they were nevertheless confined to the same discourse of backwardness. To have characterized adaptation as progressive would have been an admission of the observers' specious ideological constructions.

The following section is a short exploration of different kinds of adaptation and cross-cultural entanglement in the material culture that European observers collected, with a particular focus on the mimicry of form, which best serves to counter the idea that authenticity entails some romanticized construction of cultural purity. The reasons the objects were collected vary from cases of the collector's blindsightedness to instances in which collectors were forced to acquire things they did not want so that they could also acquire things they did want.

Kimberley Glass Points

Glass and ceramic spear points manufactured by the Aboriginal people of the Kimberley region of northwest Western Australia are visually stunning examples of cross-cultural impact. Collectors' records are almost always scant, and details on the makers, particularly in the colonial period, were rarely noted. Thus, what the skilled craftsmen who made the objects thought of them is largely a matter of conjecture. Nevertheless, there are good reasons to believe that the Aboriginal people who made these pieces placed a high value on them. Kimberley glass points have been found as far away as 1,875 miles from their source, suggesting their high trade value. Obtaining the glass to make spear points, often illegally, could actually involve serious risk for an Aboriginal person. Catriona Fisk and I have been able to uncover fourteen incidents during the period between 1860 and 1939 in which Aboriginal people were officially recorded as having been punished for vandalism or theft of material from the Overland Telegraph Line; of the sixty-one Aboriginal people punished, fifty-seven received prison sentences.[13] The craftsmen clearly considered it worth risking their freedom—and sometimes their lives—for these remarkable objects.

Drawing on Michael Taussig's work on mimicry and colonialism, Rodney Harrison has argued that glass points can be seen as the makers' attempts to imitate their own culture; reproducing stone points in glass was an expression of identity through imitation.[14] Given the risks inherent in obtaining glass insulators from telegraph lines, the production and sale of these pieces to collectors may also have been an expression of resistance against colonial authorities.

Harrison argues that the collection of these "bifacially pressure-flaked [spear] points from the Kimberley region" demonstrate cultural bias and a captivation with the aesthetics of the material that led to a kind of collector's blindsight.[15] Collectors sought these objects as examples of ingenious artistic creations of a Stone Age culture, without seeing that the material used is in fact a product of the Industrial Age.

Although the term "Kimberley point" is sometimes applied to any glass spear point made by an Aboriginal person, regardless of regional origin or method of manufacture, it refers more specifically to spear points from the Kimberley region. Stone or glass is shaped by percussive flaking with a sharp tool—such as a stone, bone, tooth, or piece of glass—to refine the edges into minute denticulate margins. The points shown in **figure 24** are made of bottle glass; in **figure 25**, ceramic.[16] According to archaeologist Kim Akerman, a noted specialist on the Aboriginal people of the Kimberley region, "stone points demand a more complex reduction sequence than glass ones."[17] Not everyone agrees, however, that the introduction of industrially manufactured materials made the process easier. Anthropologist A. P. Elkin observes that "the whole process takes hours of constant and concentrated effort, with much skill and patience. It includes the preliminary knapping of the core, which is followed by

Fig. 24 Glass points. Murchison district, Kimberley region, Western Australia, 1908. Glass. Image courtesy of the Penn Museum, Image no. 195217, 31-33-101 (Cat. 33), 31-33-104 (Cat. 34), and 31-33-113 (Cat. 35).

Fig. 25 Ceramic points. Forest River, Kimberley region, Western Australia; Murchison district, Kimberley region, Western Australia, 1906. Porcelain. Image courtesy of the Penn Museum, Image no. 255-130, 31-33-116 (Cat. 36) and 31-33-76 (Cat. 37).

the chipping or knocking-off of flakes to reduce the core to the approximate size and shape required, with a semblance of edges. The third stage consists of pressure flaking, mainly with a thicker and softer-pointed instrument, while in the fourth stage only a very sharp-pointed instrument is used."[18] Edward T. Hardman, however, claims that the creation of a glass point "did not occupy more than a half hour."[19] Although it may be that the makers adopted glass as a "raw" material because it was easier to use, other factors may be involved—the practical scavenging of whatever material was available, the beauty of the glass itself, or even a fascination with its cultural origins.

The specious Victorian-era premise that Australian Aboriginal people were Stone Age people was so tenacious that in 1890 R. Etheridge—in a statement dangerously close to absurdity—compared Kimberley glass points to "any similar productions of the Palaeolithic Period of the Old World."[20] Of course, the points are made with Industrial Age material, not material trapped in the Stone Age of technological development. Because the only difference in the points is the material employed, the objects aptly show the cultural entanglements of the frontier. That observers could not see this, instead reifying the objects as the very things they were not, shows the inherent flaws in the material basis for the conception of so-called primitive peoples as Stone Age relics. Production of glass points has greatly diminished, but Aboriginal people in some communities still continue to manufacture them. Even though the material is not indigenous, the points are fundamentally objects of Aboriginal material culture.

The Spencer and Gillen Expedition, 1901–1902

W. Baldwin Spencer and Francis James Gillen's collection at the American Museum of Natural History consists of eighty-eight separate listings, some of which include multiple objects, gathered by the pair between 1901 and 1902 on their third expedition. They first met on a scientific expedition to study the natural history of Central Australia in 1894 and worked together again in 1896–1897 on the field research that would become *Native Tribes of Central Australia* (1899).[21] The 1901–1902 expedition is especially interesting because Spencer and Gillen followed South Australia's mammoth Overland Telegraph Line from Oodnadatta in South Australia to Borroloola on the Gulf of Carpentaria (now under the jurisdiction of the Northern Territory). The telegraph route provided the insulation caps that were eventually traded between Aboriginal groups, raw material that ended up as Kimberley points. The telegraph line came about as part of an intense colonial rivalry between the states of Queensland and South Australia to secure a port as the ultimate destination of a submarine cable from Britain.[22] Although Queensland was the first to complete its telegraph line, South Australia won the connection to the mother country. Telegraph communications became possible between Adelaide and London in 1872, making the completion of the Overland Telegraph Line—a distance of 3,200 kilometers from Adelaide to the Port of Darwin—a monumental achievement.

By the time Spencer and Gillen were on their third expedition, the completed line had been in place for nearly three decades. This fact seems to have been lost on Spencer in his critique of the ethnographic work of Walter Edmund Roth, whom he had derided as only working with Aboriginal people exposed to civilization. Roth had most frequently dealt with Aboriginal people in mission and pastoral stations, but the "howling savages" of Spencer's imagination were also no strangers to the sight of European intrusions and technology. The construction bifurcated the territories through which the telegraph line intruded and eventually led to the growth of European settlement and increased conflict throughout Aboriginal land.[23] Spencer and Gillen did much of their research while stopping at the stations along the overland telegraph route.

The American Museum of Natural History's acquisition is only a small part of the enormous collection that Spencer and Gillen obtained from an exchange in 1903 of what Spencer hoped would be an equally representational collection of Northwest Coast Native American artifacts. A letter from Spencer to Boas on December 22, 1902, describes the exchange and its significance in detail:

Dear Sir,

A little time before I left Melbourne at the beginning of 1901 to spend a year amongst the Central Australian aborigines I received a letter from you written in consequence of one from myself to Professor Osborne. In this letter was expressed the desire of securing a collection of objects from the Center of Australia & offered to exchange with us.

I am now sending you a series which fairly well represents those used by our Central Australian tribes.

The most important amongst them is a Nurtunja with attached churinga which is similar to one of the same object as described by Mr. Gillen & myself in the "Native Tribes of Central Australia." In addition to this which is most difficult to procure there are smaller objects which will doubtless be of interest to you. Unfortunately in regard to our Australian things there is very little which is "showy" from a public point of view but many of the specimens included in this collection are very difficult to secure & such things as the "tana" & "churinga" (except they be made for sale as they soon will be) are only obtainable by those who know the natives intimately. One unfortunate resulting [sic] the work of Mr. Gillen & myself has been the revealing of the fact that such articles as "churinga" have a marketable value & as a natural result they are now sought after by the white men and already the natives are beginning to manufacture them. The South Australian Government is now preparing to build a railway across the centre of the continent & as a result of this we shall [see] a large number of native implements etc. sent down which be put about as genuine as [they are] now offered for sale in south Africa or at railway stations as one crosses America.

Everything in your collection is genuine. The only doubtful things are the fire-sticks from the Arunta tribe & the only non-native thing about these is that the sticks were cut with knives. There were very few fire-sticks in the sample and as I was anxious to secure them the natives made them for me and in each case I saw them actually used for the purpose of "making fire" so that they are really genuine.

Can you help me to secure a Totem pole such as Dr. Taylor has in the Oxford Museum? I do not know how far it is possible to obtain this or whether it is possible at all but I am most anxious to have something which is typical of "totemism" in America just as the Nurtunja with its churinga is typical of our Australian totemic groups.

If you desire any further particulars about the specimens sent I should be glad to provide you with these but I think that you will get such information as you desire either in our last book or in the one which will I hope very soon be published.

Yours very sincerely,

W. Baldwin Spencer[24]

Spencer detested objects that showed "degeneration" or admixture of cultures, and in some cases records of such entanglements were actively eradicated from his collection. For example, knowing his distaste for objects showing Aboriginal use of European materials, some of Spencer's collection agents would replace iron adze heads with flint ones, effectively manufacturing false "authenticity."[25] Despite his having declared to Boas that the only possibly inauthentic objects in his collection were the Yanyuwa (Anula) fire sticks made with metal knives, Spencer either failed to notice or chose to ignore the use of a metal hoop in the construction of at least one other object **(fig. 26)**. In his list for the museum, Spencer gives a short but informative description:

> Arunta Tribe
> Macarthur River
> *Locality* Gulf of Carpentaria
> Entry 51:
> Smoking pipe. Anula and Mara Tribes. This is only met with amongst the tribes on the gulf coast. The Central tribes have no pipe, and this pipe is only used for smoking trade tobacco. Probably derived from the Malays, with whom the coastal tribes come into contact.

The metal hoop embedded in the pipe to serve as a tobacco bowl is not mentioned in the object notes or description. Despite Spencer's having noted that the object is "for smoking trade tobacco," the piece is not included in his list of "doubtful things."

Trade tobacco, along with this characteristic pipe, probably penetrated the northern coast of Australia through Macassan traders. Smoking tobacco caught on very quickly in Australia—and in much of the Pacific—and tobacco was frequently used as a trade good in interactions with native populations.

Fig. 26 Pipe. Arunta culture, Central Australia, Northern Territory, Australia, late 19th century. Wood, pigment; metal, plant fiber, soot. Courtesy of the Division of Anthropology, American Museum of Natural History, ST/4179 (Cat. 21).

Fig. 27 Pipe. Yolgnu culture, Elcho Island, Arnhem Land, Northern Territory, Australia, mid-20th century. Wood, pigment; metal, soot. Courtesy of the Division of Anthropology, American Museum of Natural History, 80.1/3670 (Cat. 22).

Figure 27 shows a slightly later pipe that anthropologist Ronald Berndt (1916–1990) collected from Elcho Island in the Northern Territory in the first half of the twentieth century. The pipe shows less elaboration than the one collected by Spencer and Gillen, although both have traces of tobacco indicating their use as smoking implements. In Queensland and Central Australia, tobacco began to replace the indigenous pituri plant, which has a high nicotine content. According to Roth, "among the aboriginals themselves every-where as great a craving appears to exist for pituri as alcohol for Europeans. . . . Mr. Reardon, the manager at Carlo, tells me that when on the Mulligan the supply of tobacco runs out the aboriginals will smoke pituri in their pipes."[26] Pituri was usually chewed, so the introduction of tobacco may have changed the way the local drug was used. The number of tobacco pipes in muse-um collections certainly indicates tobacco's popularity among Aboriginal people in colonial times. Even today, consumption is proportionally higher among Aboriginal Australians than it is in European Australian communities.

Pipe smoking became an important fea-ture of Aboriginal diplomatic customs.[27] In his 1896 report on the Queensland Aborigines, Meston wrote about the importance of tobacco to Aboriginal communities. When the Reverend Nicholas Hey banned its use in his mission station, Meston lamented: "No man loathes tobacco in every shape more than I do, but my opinion is not in favour of withholding it from the aboriginal, certainly not from those who have once acquired the habit. Introduced among wild tribes it is a potent pacificator and a valuable social agent. Their enjoyments are few, and as one vice having apparently no seriously bad effect they may be allowed to smoke their 'calumet of peace' without restraint."[28]

Finsch also collected a number of tobacco pipes and samples of both native and trade tobacco, and his wife painted a watercolor depicting New Guineans smoking trade tobacco in pipes **(fig. 28)**. In addition, one of his photographs shows men and women from Matupi in the Bismarck Archipelago, two of whom have European-style pipes in their mouths, an image that upsets Finsch's otherwise carefully constructed depiction of an untouched society **(fig. 29)**.

Mimetic Things

Nearly half a century after Finsch, Margaret Mead (1901–1978) traveled to New Guinea and also collected at least one tobacco pipe for the American Museum of Natural History **(fig. 30)**. The pipe is particularly fascinating because it is not a functional object. Mead left scant notes on the object, only a simple description, "964. imitation of a child's pipe made by a child," and the location of its collection, Mount Arapesh, where she and Reo Fortune (1903–1979) spent eight months conducting research. The people of Mount Arapesh have no name for themselves, and the word *arapesh* itself roughly means "people." Arapesh country covers diverse territory, including coastal regions, inland plains, foothills, and mountains. The local language is

Fig. 28 Otto and Elisabeth Finsch. New Guinea locals smoking tobacco pipes, late 19th century. Watercolor. Papers of Otto Finsch, accession file 1898-49. Courtesy of the Division of Anthropology, American Museum of Natural History.

Fig. 29 Men and women from Matupi Island, 1884–1885. Papers of Otto Finsch, accession file 1898-49. Courtesy of the Division of Anthropology, American Museum of Natural History.

Fig. 30 Child's imitation pipe. Arapesh culture, Aitape district, Papua New Guinea, early 20th century. Reed wood. Courtesy of the Division of Anthropology, American Museum of Natural History, 80.0/6981 (Cat. 23).

not commonly used anymore, having given way to Tok Pisin, a creole language used throughout New Guinea. By the 1930s, when Mead and Fortune were living there, European visitors—often missionaries—were commonplace. Trade goods had penetrated into the territory and local populations were integrated into nearby plantations. The pipe, part of Mead's 1933 acquisition for the museum, is constructed from two pieces of wood: the carved bowl and the reed, which is fixed without any adhesive material into a narrow perforation in the bowl. This piece is an intriguing example of a mimetic object, made to resemble a European pipe, but not functional as one. Instead, it is a child's toy that, judging from Mead's notes, was actually made by a child. An unhealthy toy to modern eyes perhaps, but one that raises the interesting question of whether the child was imitating a local smoker's pipe or one belonging to a European.

A noteworthy collection of artifacts from the New Hebrides (Vanuatu) at the American Museum of Natural History also contains imitative objects. The collector, James H. Lawrie (1850–1921), lived as a missionary in the Vanuatu region for seventeen years **(fig. 31)**. In *The New Hebrides and Christian Missions* (1880), Robert Steel presents him as one of the "new missionaries" who would

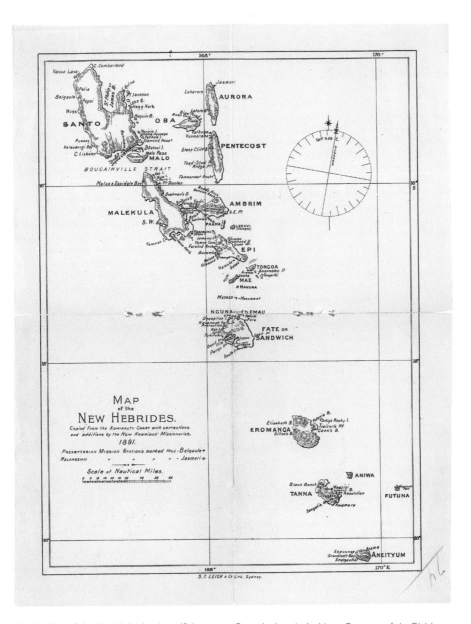

Fig. 31 Map of the New Hebrides. Late 19th century. From the Lawrie Archives. Courtesy of the Division of Anthropology, American Museum of Natural History.

make up for his predecessors' lack of zeal. He expected Lawrie to "exercise a wholesome influence, by means of discipline and Christian instruction," and to "lead [his congregation] further into Christian life."[29] Despite Steel's positive estimate of the future spiritual health of the region, the book was very much in line with conventional racial discourse on the slow doom encompassing the non-European inhabitants of the Pacific. Disease, Steel reports, was rapidly diminishing the native population.[30] Lawrie also believed that the local culture in the area was being radically changed by the process of colonialism. He wrote to the museum in September 1895, offering part of his collection: "In compliance with the promise made to you in the end of July—I now forward as per enclosed list, specimens of all the New Hebridean Curios that I can spare from my private Collection. Many of these artifacts are now difficult to obtain owing to the increased intercourse with Europeans and the consequent change in native customs and industries."[31]

Lawrie's collection at the museum contains 135 objects, encompassing a wide variety of ethnological artifacts, including raw material, such as breadfruit wood, bark that Ni-Vanuatu women used in the manufacture of tapa cloth, and specimens of roots that people in Aneityum (the southernmost island of Vanuatu) once used in sun worship. Weapons of war and hunting are also well represented by several sets of bows and arrows, clubs, slings, and spear throwers. Finally, there are other objects that the Ni-Vanuatu commonly used for utilitarian and ornamental purposes: shellfish hooks, pandanus leaf baskets, decorative combs, turtle shell carvings, headrests, and whale teeth. These goods were sent onboard the steamship *Principia* from Leith in Scotland, where Lawrie had returned, for a total of thirty-three pounds sterling, twenty pounds of which had been paid by Lawrie as insurance on the collection. The Museum's curator of Mexican archaeology, M. H. Saville, was involved in acquiring the collection, despite it being beyond his own regional specialization. He enthusiastically endorsed the acquisition, declaring that "this collection of 135 specimens . . . cannot be duplicated for many times the amount for which it is insured."[32]

Lawrie's collection includes one last piece of clearly imitative and deeply entangled style and material, a woman's bonnet **(fig. 32)**. Although the artifact did not rank highly enough to receive mention in the Museum's 1910 report to the trustees, the bonnet, from the island of Aneityum, is now catalogued in the American Museum of Natural History's collection. Museum records indicate the bonnet might have been from the island of Efate, now the most populous of the islands of Vanuatu. With its bays and inlets, and much level terrain suitable for comfortable living, Efate was one of the earliest islands of Vanuatu to

Fig. 32 Woman's bonnet. Ni-Vanuatu culture, Aneityum, Vanuatu, late 19th century. Pandanus leaf, cotton, silk ribbon, newspaper. Courtesy of the Division of Anthropology, American Museum of Natural History, ST/3267 (Cat. 29).

Fig. 33 Interior detail of Fig. 32.

receive missionary attention. Nevertheless, the object is stylistically consistent with other such poke bonnets made in Aneityum, and there appear to be no collection records to confirm any strong connection with Efate. Lawrie provides little detail about the bonnet, only listing it as "1 Native made Woman's bonnet" in the inventory he supplied with his collection. It is one of the more interesting examples of the "increased intercourse with Europeans." He claims that "many of these objects are now difficult to obtain" but fails to recognize the emerging complexity of Ni-Vanuatu creations evident in the artifact. Although it is clearly identified as having been made by a Ni-Vanuatu, most of the materials in the piece are not of local origin. The bonnet does include twine made from indigenous plant fiber, but it also includes at least four varieties of commercially manufactured cloth on the exterior: the red rim, two green-and-gray streamers or ribbons on each side, and a red-and-yellow patterned cloth around the crown. Perhaps of greater interest is the inner construction of the bonnet, which again uses multicolored cloth. The underside of the crown is padded with newspaper, sewn in as lining to provide the structure necessary to imitate European bonnets **(fig. 33)**.

The text of the newspaper that gives shape to the bonnet is still readable, providing a tantalizing glimpse at the context in which the object was made. Conservation work in preparation for exhibition of the bonnet has revealed that the newspaper is from Edinburgh. The publication's name is not discernible, but the majority of the advertisements are for small businesses in the mercantile district of Leith, a port for maritime trade. Although most of the margins and many sentences are cut short, one article appears to cover a dock dispute. Because Lawrie was from Scotland, there is a chance that he was the source of the newspaper used as lining. It is evident from the stitching that the newspaper was not added after the artifact was collected, indicating that the Ni-Vanuatu woman who made the bonnet must have chosen the material. In places we can still read the text clearly: "A stevedore was charged with using lights on board a vessel in the docks, while flax was being discharged, and in the evidence which led to the conviction of the offender, a number of [obscured text] circumstances were elicited [the text is cut off]." Labor relations in late nineteenth-century Vanuatu were important because it was one of the island groups that sailors would visit to blackbird (kidnap or compel under false pretenses) able-bodied men as plantation workers, particularly for the sugarcane plantations of Queensland and Fiji.[33] In his work on the Christian missions of the New Hebrides, Steel reports that "even from this island, so difficult to access, and with a small population, one hundred and nine natives were taken away in three years by the labour vessels from Fiji and Queensland. Of these, fourteen died, and twelve were killed during their absence from the island. There were twenty-eight away in 1874, and of these, two had been absent for seven years; and eight had been taken away, and six returned, during the same year."[34]

The material used in this example of cross-cultural entanglement in Oceania is predominantly of commercial manufacture, repurposed for a "Native made Woman's bonnet" that incorporates a record of the imposition of colonial law and labor on a community that was one of many subject to the unequal distribution of both. The bonnet is also imitative, combining imported material with local plant fiber to fashion a European woman's headpiece. Clothing in Vanuatu had been (and still is) an important part of individual and communal identity. Traders and missionaries who visited or settled in the islands introduced European clothing to the islands, and as the missionaries sought to convert the local populace, wearing European-style clothing became a visible sign of conversion.[35]

Introduced clothing styles brought some social changes to the Ni-Vanuatu. On the one hand, European clothing could disguise class differences that were otherwise made apparent by tattoos. On the other hand, for those who adopted European clothing, the more frequent washing and repair work that commercial cloth required compared to local textiles changed the nature of female labor.[36] Wearing introduced clothing to indicate higher status was not confined to the Ni-Vanuatu; indeed, the phenomenon had been prevalent since early trade contacts. In the eighteenth-century Pacific, for example, officer's tricorns and soldier's coats were desirable objects for islanders because they signified a relationship with powerful people.[37]

The Ni-Vanuatu quickly adopted European-style clothing, reproduced from local and foreign materials. Bonnets such as the one in Lawrie's collection were part of a woman's clothing for Christian rituals. H. A. Robertson, a missionary on Erromango from 1872 to 1913, offers an account of clothing from the same region that describes a similar piece:

> The women . . . wore, and do still wear, skirts made of the pandanus leaf. A great number of these are donned at one time, one over another, and as they are fairly short, just reaching to the knees, they give their wearers a queer, bunchy appearance. These skirts, with the addition of a short print jacket, formed a woman[']s week-day attire; while on Sundays, and on all state occasions, a wonderful head-gear, in the form of a large barrel-shaped bonnet made of plaited [ ] pandanus leaf, surmounted all. These bonnets were cut into shape and sewed by Esther. The hair on the women's heads being thick and woolly, the bonnets were usually worn on their shoulders, the strings being tied securely in front, and the Aneityumese belle thus equipped was, to herself and her admirers, a thing of beauty. The men, as Christians, were clad in shirts and short kilts or lava-lava, no covering being worn on their heads.[38]

Such objects, especially if worn by a local, could make defining cultural boundaries problematic for those with a vested interest in doing so. As objects of obvious mimicry, the bonnets may have even played a part in European anxieties over miscegenation. Although the mixture of indigenous and commercial materials may have led Lawrie to narrowly construe the Ni-Vanuatu bonnet as inauthentic, the piece is in fact a product of complex social and material interactions in the colonial Pacific world. The subject matter of the newspaper lining may even tempt one to ask whether this object may have been intended in some way as a subversive or defiant symbol. Given that English was a language of missionary instruction in British territories, it is possible that the woman who made this bonnet was able to read the newsprint she used for lining. If so, the lining may have been one of Scott's "hidden transcripts."

Notes

1   Aird, "Growing Up with Aborigines," 23.
2   Ibid., 25.
3   Scott, *Domination and the Arts of Resistance*.
4   Meston, "The Evolution of the Boomerang: Part I."
5   McGregor, "The Doomed Race."
6   See Khan, *Catalogue of the Roth Collection*, 1:13.
7   Although the "wilderness" is very much a European concept, I use it to evoke the settlers' conceptualization of the frontier. A wilderness is, by definition, an unsettled and uncultivated region. The presence of Aboriginal people on the frontier meant that an Australian "wilderness" did not actually exist.
8   See Rowse, *White Flour, White Power*, 14.
9   Fison and Howitt, *Kamilaroi and Kurnai*.
10   Ibid., 181.
11   Ibid., 181–182.
12   Cleland, "President's Address."
13   Rowlands and Fisk, "'A Dearly Bought Amusement.'"
14   Harrison, "The Magical Virtue of These Sharp Things," 311–336. See also Taussig, *Mimesis and Alterity*.
15   Harrison, "An Artefact of Colonial Desire?"
16   For a fuller explanation of these pieces and others, see Rowlands and Fisk, "Broken Glass."
17   Akerman, "On Kimberley Points and the Politics of Enchantment," 133.
18   Elkin, "Pressure Flaking in Northern Kimberley, Australia," 112.
19   Hardman, "Notes on a Collection of Native Weapons and Implements," 58.
20   Etheridge, "On Some Beautifully-Formed Stone Spear-Heads," 61.
21   The expedition went by train from Adelaide to Oodnadatta in South Australia, then though Central Australia by camel to the Macdonnell ranges in the Northern Territory. Spencer and Gillen, *The Native Tribes of Central Australia*.
22   See Pike, "The Northern Territory Overland Telegraph," 97.
23   See, for example, "Stealing Telegraph Wires," *Kiama Independent and Shoalhaven Advertiser*, April 19, 1887, 4.
24   Spencer to Boas, December 22, 1902, Papers of W. Baldwin Spencer, accession file 1903-14, Division of Anthropology, AMNH.
25   See Mulvaney, "Annexing All I Can Lay Hands On," 147.
26   Walter Edmund Roth, *Ethnological Studies among the North-West-Central Queensland Aborigines*, 100.
27   See Basedow, *The Australian Aboriginal*, 156.
28   Meston, *Report on the Aboriginals of Queensland*.
29   Steel, *The New Hebrides and Christian Missions*, 127.
30   Ibid.
31   Lawrie to the Museum, September 25, 1895, Papers of James H. Lawrie, accession file

1896-18, Division of Anthropology, AMNH.

32 Saville to the Museum, October 5, 1895,
    Papers of James H. Lawrie, accession file
    1896-18, Division of Anthropology, AMNH.

33 It is impossible to do justice to the enormous
    topic of blackbirding in these pages; for a
    starting point, see Mortensen's "Slaving in
    Australian Courts."

34 Steel, *The New Hebrides and Christian
    Missions*, 144.

35 See Bolton, "Gender, Status and Introduced
    Clothing in Vanuatu," 121, 128.

36 Ibid., 128–132.

37 See Newell, "Collecting from the Collectors,"
    35.

38 See Robertson, *Erromanga*, 101.

Conclusion
"Proper Ones Would Be Much Better"

The collections discussed in *Frontier Shores* share the common trait of having been acquired by, or specifically for, museums. Although they may not have seen themselves as professional natural scientists interested in cataloguing human archetypes, as Spencer and Finsch did, none of the collectors saw the material they gathered as unimportant. Positioning the collections within mainstream scientific thought concerning the inadaptability of indigenous technologies meant that the human beings who belonged to the cultures studied were likewise positioned as pedagogical tools.

Collection is a conscious attempt to make meaning through categorization. The emphasis on classification removes objects from their original context and places them "into relationships . . . by seriality"; thus, according to S. M. Pearce, collections are formed through "the imposition of ideas of classification and seriality on the external world."[1] Object acquisition constitutes a deliberate attempt to understand the world and to place some order on it. Ethnographic collections in museums attempt to explain and categorize cultures. More than mere displays of objects, they are assemblages of human possessions, experiences, and attitudes. But does a collection reflect what the collector intended, or is it merely an imaginary construct? Colonial fieldworkers sought to study untouched "native" culture and to document and explain the patterns of behavior they observed.[2] *Frontier Shores* has discussed flaws in the interpretation of the material and cultural elements in such collections. The traditions that observers sought to record were narrowly defined by colonial-era rhetoric and political convenience. Indeed, the narrative that collectors sought to construct can be seen as a kind of hyperreality resulting from a failure to distinguish representations of a thing from the thing itself.[3]

Colonial collections were not merely confined to physical objects; they were also ideological and metaphysical (Christian missionaries, for instance, were collecting souls in Oceania). Physical collections include not only the visible but the invisible as well. Semioticians would term the invisible parts of a collection "unspoken signs" that catalogue and categorize, composing conceptions of types, cultures, and themes. Because it cannot so easily be collected, intangible heritage, such as ceremony, dance, and performance, does not generally form part of a culture's material record. Although the means were relatively limited during the colonial period, technological advances in sound and image recording expanded the range of collection. The hyperreality of early twentieth-century ethnography can be found in an early instance of the acquisition of "invisible" material.

Recording Performance

Four phonographic recordings, which eminent Austrian anthropologist Felix von Luschan (1854–1924) made in 1914, represent a unique capturing of a relatively intangible manifestation of an Aboriginal culture. The year marked the arrival of the British Association for the Advancement of Science in Australia—a major coup for former colonies that sought to be taken seriously in the scientific world. Luschan was one of the few guests from outside the British Empire. Although he was certainly no stranger to the mainstream collection of human data in the form of human remains, anthropometric measurements, and material culture, his brief work in Australia put him on the cutting edge of anthropological research.

Audio recordings of voices, songs, and ceremonies were difficult to gather because the equipment required was expensive and cumbersome. Early phonographs used cylinders that were rotated by either an internal motor or a hand crank at a steady speed to create recordings or to play them back. In addition, a horn—often made from brass, wood, or glass—was required to amplify the sound. Although disks were often used, cylinders offered the greatest fidelity because their shape provided a more consistent surface velocity. The recordings from early phonographs are, of course, very limited compared to those produced by later technologies. Nevertheless, they presented a completely unparalleled means of representing experiences that were otherwise transient or intangible.[4]

The four-inch wax cylinders **(fig. 34)** that Luschan used could usually only record a few minutes of sound, thus limiting their capacity for capturing ceremonies.[5] His recordings, running for less than a minute each, represent only a small sample of the ceremony. Recording multiple voices was also problematic,

Fig. 34 Wax cylinders and cylinder boxes from the Luschan collections of the Berlin Phonogram Archive. Early 20th century. Original cylinder (light brown), Galvano (copper negative), old copy (black), new copy (red). © Ethnologisches Museum, Staatliche Museen zu Berlin–Preussischer Kulturbesitz. Photograph: Christiane Siegert, 2005.

but quite remarkably, Luschan's four recordings contain more than one voice (usually two), and one even includes the sound of a boomerang being used as a clap stick to keep rhythm.[6] Despite the limitations of the technology, Luschan was able to stage, with the assistance of Wurundjeri performers, a sort of representational or simulated performance.

Luschan made the recordings in the Wurundjeri settlement of Coranderrk, near Healesville in rural Victoria, a much-beleaguered refuge whose population had drastically shrunk as a result of the Aborigines Protection Act of 1886, which evicted those the state defined as half-caste, under the age of thirty-five, from the land. The community had persisted under hardship, continuing to perform ceremonies, even after the loss of much of their working population and some of their most arable land.[7] The Wurundjeri may have seen the visit of the British Association for the Advancement of Science as a major though brief distraction. Luschan had been advised in writing by a missionary at Coranderrk that the Wurundjeri would enjoy singing into the gramophone and being recorded.[8] Although a handful of their recorded voices are available for listening, we have no record of how they actually felt about the exercise or whether they believed they were making a faithful version of their songs for the German ethnographer. Whether they were aware of the growing tensions between Luschan and many of the other scientists is unknown, but it is interesting to speculate on whether the Wurundjeri would have empathized with him as a fellow "other" in relation to mainstream British Australia.[9]

At Coranderrk, the Wurundjeri sometimes conducted corroborees,[10] which were performed for differing reasons depending on the audience. Jane Lydon discusses two performances in the community, both earlier than those Luschan recorded.[11] In 1890, a corroboree was held at a local Christian wedding, largely for the purpose of entertainment. In 1898, a corroboree was staged for a European photographer who only partially succeeded in getting the participants to dress down for their roles and, as Lydon observes, could not gather enthusiasm enough for more than a mechanical performance. We cannot know from Luschan's notes exactly what kind of corroboree he was recording or whether it was met with much enthusiasm. Although Luschan was using modern technology to record a supposedly "ancient" performance, what he actually recorded is a representation of a local one. It would be shortsighted, however, to treat this performance as some sort of farce. In all likelihood, Luschan would have been aware of the entanglement of technology and simulation and was merely making do with the materials he had. The participants would in turn most likely have intended their performance to be a faithful rendition of what they would normally do on a larger scale, with more performers, and in more fluid motion than standing around a gramophone allows.

As a result of tensions following the outbreak of the Great War, Luschan had to flee the country with his wife shortly after visiting Coranderrk, which may account for the brevity of his usually meticulous notes. He did not manage to date the recordings or identify their precise location. When they fled, the Luschans had to leave unused cylinders behind, which they had to explain to a most probably sympathetic Erich Moritz von Hornbostel, who had loaned them the recording equipment from the Berlin Phonogram Archive.

Jane Goodale and the Tiwi Islanders

Much later, and much farther north, a National Geographic expedition to the Tiwi Islands (Melville and Bathurst Islands in the Northern Territory) in 1954 resulted in a similar collection of conscious representations by Aboriginal people. Among the anthropologists was Jane Goodale (1926–2008), then a doctoral student from the United States. Goodale remained behind eight months longer than her fellows to conduct the fieldwork component of her dissertation. Because they were island dwellers, the Tiwi were less accessible than many other Aboriginal

Australians; even so, they were not strangers to ethnographic research. In 1928 and 1929, C. W. M. Hart (1905–1976) visited the Tiwi Islands, as did Arnold R. Pilling in 1953–1954. Hart and Pilling eventually collaborated on a book about the Tiwi that covers both time periods they observed, focusing extensively on the role of marriage in Tiwi society.[12]

Goodale's stay with the Tiwi Islanders led to a series of rich anthropological works as well as the acquisition of a significant collection of material culture for the University of Pennsylvania Museum of Archaeology and Anthropology. Toward the end of her stay, Goodale asked a local man, Paddy Nonolu, whether he could help her acquire objects for the museum. She recorded this encounter in detail:

> You know I shall be leaving in a few months' time, and that the museum in America where I work has asked me to collect spears, baskets, pandanus arm bands, dance clubs, stone axes, and all the things which the Tiwi make, so that they can put them where Americans can see them. Now I think they would also like to see some of the funeral poles, but these are only made for a funeral and are put up around the grave to stay forever. I can't take them away from a grave. Do you think you could make me some little toy ones so that they could see what they are like?[13]

Paddy Nonolu asked if Goodale would prefer "more better big ones," and she replied: "Of course . . . proper ones would be much better."[14]

Although Tiwi mortuary poles conform to general shapes and sizes, they are created individually, so no two are alike. Called *pukumani*, the poles are carved from single pieces of wood and stand—even with their base buried in earth—seven or eight feet tall. They are part of an elaborate and prolonged ritual that begins weeks after the burial of a deceased member of the community. The islanders selected to carve the poles are chosen because they have a kinship relationship with the deceased. Both women and men carve the poles, but the carvers are more often men because of the intensive physical labor involved.[15] The carver's imagination is a powerful factor in creating a pole—limited only by the dimensions of the tree and the required patterns of yellow, red, and white colors and charcoal **(fig. 35)**. Once the poles are finished, they are raised around the grave of the deceased **(fig. 36)**. The community gathers at the gravesite for a dance ceremony. The dancers are daubed in pigment, in colors and patterns that remove any semblance of individual identity, so as to confuse the spirits of

Fig. 35 Tiwi Islanders pigmenting a *pukumani* (mortuary pole). Mid-20th century. Image courtesy of the Penn Museum, image no. 255124.

the dead and prevent ghosts from abducting the living and "carrying them off into the densest part of the bush and making them insensible and eventually killing them."[16]

Pukumani were most commonly left near the gravesite once their ritual purpose was complete. Because they were constructed of wood, the elements and the termites would quickly destroy them. Today, the poles are commonly sold to collectors and museums after they have served their purpose, for such traditions adapt to the needs and desires of the community and to the world they live in. When Goodale commissioned a series of eight poles, however, the pukumani would normally have been allowed to decay following their ritual use. The Tiwi Islanders who made the pieces were aware that they were not intended for eventual use in Goodale's own funeral. Goodale made it clear that she was collecting them for the Pennsylvania museum, not for personal use. The eight poles were in fact too short—by a foot—to serve as "authentic" pukumani. Thus, although the poles were modeled on authentic funerary pieces, the Tiwi Islanders were most likely also aware that the objects were staged representations.

In the same year that Goodale commissioned the pukumani, a Tiwi artist known as "short Katu" made one for presentation to Queen Elizabeth II. The pole had a carved human figure atop the post that Katu had created after being inspired by the human statuary he saw in Darwin.[17] Spencer would no doubt have written off such pukumani as examples of "admixture" or "degeneration" and would have been further horrified to learn that they had been carved with metal tools. The poles do, of course, demonstrate the extent to which Tiwi Islanders had adopted European tools and stylistic influences. The tools had changed by Goodale's time, and the Tiwi understood that, as museum pieces, the poles were re-creations of traditional ceremonial objects. Because the pukumani, as absolutely faithful creations, should be considered authentic, they fit somewhat ambiguously into the category of simulated objects. Indeed, for Goodale a sense of their authenticity endured: "When I left Melville Island in December I said *nimbangi* [farewell] to all the ghosts as well as to the living Tiwi, but I cannot look at the poles which now rest in the Museum without feeling that I was followed by the Tiwi, who will always dance and sing for me beside the painted poles."[18]

With the benefit of operating at a later date than the other collectors discussed in these pages, Goodale may have been well aware that elements of European and Aboriginal culture were entangled in everyday lives. She observed countless instances of entanglement in the tools people used, the language they spoke, and even in the gambling incorporated into Tiwi women's daily work. Goodale did not consider the people she studied inauthentic or degenerate because they did not inhabit some reified "pure" culture. But her perspective cannot simply be ascribed to her arriving in the Tiwi Islands in the mid-twentieth century. After all, the longest-serving Protector of Queensland Aborigines, J. W. Bleakley (1879–1957), wrote in the introduction to his *Aborigines of Australia*—first published in 1961, only half a decade after Goodale's stay with the Tiwi—that Aboriginal people were "perhaps the last human relics of the Stone Age."[19] In a classic piece of paternalistic racism, Bleakley supposes that "whether the [Queensland] aborigines . . . will ever arrive at the stage of development when they will cease to need their present benevolent supervision and help and become happily assimilated in the community only time will tell. Probably they will need paternal care as long as any remnants of the full-bloods are left."[20] Bleakley's views may be regarded as reflections of long-past attitudes, a result of his being much older than Goodale, or of having made his career as a government official, not an anthropologist.

Fig. 36 Tiwi Islanders erecting a *pukumani* (mortuary pole). Mid-20th century. Image courtesy of the Penn Museum, image no. 255125.

As a counter to the idea that such views are simply reflections of long-past attitudes, consider Jimmy Nelson's *Before They Pass Away*, a photographic record of "indigenous" peoples that the author believes are in danger of vanishing into history. Nelson's website for the book describes his objective: "In 2009, I planned to become a guest of 31 secluded and visually unique tribes. I wanted to witness their time-honoured traditions, join in their rituals and discover how the rest of the world is threatening to change their way of life forever. Most importantly, I wanted to create an ambitious aesthetic photographic document that would stand the test of time. A body of work that would be an irreplaceable ethnographic record of a fast disappearing world." Nelson explains that "the detail that is attained by using [a 4 × 5 plate camera] would provide an extraordinary view into the emotional and spiritual lives of the last indigenous peoples of the world. At the same time, it would glorify their varying and unique cultural creativity with their painted faces, scarified bodies, jewellery, extravagant hairstyles and ritual language."[21] Nelson's claim that the thirty-one secluded tribes he visited (by his own admission, for a period not exceeding two weeks per tribe) are the "last indigenous peoples of the world" is, of course, untenable. The discussion of entanglement in *Frontier Shores* is intended as an antidote to the notion that contact with the West leads to the cultural eradication of colonized peoples. Although there have been occasions throughout history when cultures have vanished, in the case of nineteenth- and twentieth-century Oceania the adoption of certain European forms, materials, and customs did not mean inescapable extinction. Such quaint notions belong to Victorian-era science.

Cultural entanglement is not an expression of the inauthentic. Inauthenticity is itself a construct of collection, colonialism, and the benevolent romanticism that beguiled European observers. Every artifact discussed in these pages is fundamentally an authentic object that individuals manufactured, using materials and representations that were relevant and active parts of their lives. Although the materials and tools may have changed over time, the changes were dictated by convenience, utility, access to resources, and a desire for or curiosity about new methods. The adoption of glass in Aboriginal spearheads did not make these people false or hybrids any more than drinking tea made the English Chinese.

Drawing on the work of psychoanalyst Jacques Lacan, Homi Bhabha treats the colonized's mimicry of the colonizer as a kind of "ambivalence." Lacan defined mimicry as being "like the technique of camouflage practised in human warfare"[22] and applied the concept to his own theory of cultural resistance in the colonial context. Ambivalence, according to Bhabha, is a form of mimicry in which the colonized adopt the cultural norms and trappings of the colonizer in a selective fashion that makes the colonized "almost the same, *but not quite,*" as their colonial masters.[23] Mimicry could also lead to a heightened sense of the "other" through the incongruity of familiarity and physical difference. Ambivalence created a compromise between cultural independence, resistance, and the need for a static and secure society.[24]

Frontier Shores has examined instances of cultural exchange between Europeans and the people of Oceania, some of which were not entirely mutual, but neither were they always rapacious. Discussing the "shock" that occurs when different cultures meet, Umberto Eco identifies three possible outcomes: conquest, cultural pillage, and exchange. He defines "exchange" as a "two-way process of reciprocal influence and respect"[25] but adds that the three terms are "abstract models, . . . in reality there are a variety of cases in which these attitudes are merged."[26] As the collections I have discussed demonstrate, late nineteenth- and early twentieth-century Oceania represents one of the "variety of cases" of cross-cultural encounter in which exchange, conquest, and pillage are themselves entangled with adaptation, ingenuity, and survivalism on the part of native people.

Collection, often a well-meaning or simply inquisitive pastime, became embroiled in the process of othering in the Pacific world. But collection alone did not create the "other"; rather, European perceptions of the imagined and the entangled frontier determined the process. Otto Finsch provides a novel example of a collector who was far ahead of his peers in thoughtful and detailed collection research, dismissive of false notions of race, and yet unable to overcome the overly simplistic notion that his collection served as evidence of a "Stone Age" culture. This notion, especially in concert with theories of racial dominance, was commonplace among Oceania collectors. The collectors sought to preserve what they saw as remnants of vanishing cultures and, sometimes, vanishing people. They reified anything that proved the suppositions of their ideological discourses. They assumed that the native people they studied were Stone Age curiosities, largely incapable of adaptation, and took the material culture that these "curiosities" created as proof. The native inhabitants of Oceania were imagined as culturally pure but stagnant, incapable of adapting to "civilized" life and therefore doomed to quickly vanish. This view was largely informed by prevailing ideas of "race" and evolution, along with a flawed interpretation of the material record, one that ignored contradictory evidence gathered in collections, particularly of "entangled" objects. Rather than providing evidence of degeneration, the entanglement of cultures in such objects disproves the entire colonial discourse on adaptation.

As Nicholas Thomas has observed, the desire for objects of encounter in the Pacific was mutual and led to a fascination (but not necessarily beguilement) with certain things.[27] Objects that demonstrate elements of mimicry provide good examples: the cutlass-shaped club (see fig. 1) suggests the maker's interest in the object he was mimicking, as does the similar Massim hand club (see fig. 13). The former is not just an imitative piece but also a faithful work of its maker's culture. In addition, more obviously imitative objects, such as the Ni-Vanuatu woman's bonnet (see figs. 32 and 33) may express a subversive intent. The Kimberley glass and ceramic points (see figs. 24 and 25) are especially clear examples of entangled objects, using material from an industrial society, repurposed to mimic more archaic objects of Aboriginal culture. Along with the element of utility (glass is easier to work with than stone), there is an ironic aspect to the material's having been traded back to Europeans, some of whom interpreted the objects as "neolithic work."[28] The spear points reinforce a local Aboriginal idea of self while subtly subverting European notions of Aboriginal identity. In the similar case of the tale of the Tongan origins of Bonaparte, Lorimer Fison dismisses the account from a European perspective, treating it as merely an example of the adoption of foreign ideas into local mythologies. He fails to see that the tale is not merely an adoption; it is in fact the storyteller's reinvention, creating a story that is more useful, palatable, and self-affirming for Tongans. The same could be said of all the entanglements discussed in *Frontier Shores*: foreign materials may have been incorporated for a variety of reasons, but ultimately because they were more useful in the evolving nature of tradition across the region.

In conclusion, I would not argue that Luschan's recordings or Goodale's Tiwi poles are examples of the hyperreal or that any of the artifacts or stories I have discussed are inauthentic or aberrations. Let me suggest instead that the element of simulation derives from colonial observers' having acquired and used artifacts to support their contention that the "indigenous other" is primordial and therefore poorly suited to the modern world. They used an analysis of material to prove what they already believed before they had observed it—that the native cultures they interacted with were stagnant and vanishing. Had they properly considered the material in their collections, they would have seen that adaptation was in fact the norm and that in the process of trying to prove their misguided notions, they had in fact failed to realize that the authenticity they sought was an illusion of their own making.

Notes

1   Pearce, "Collecting Reconsidered," 87, 88.

2   See Elkin, "Conservation of Aboriginal Peoples," 95.

3   For an exploration of the theory of hyperreality, see, for example, Baudrillard, "The Precession of Simulacra."

4   The phonograph became one of the late nineteenth-century world's enduring symbols of technological marvel and progress. Indeed, it features as one of the means by which the characters in Bram Stoker's *Dracula* (1897) record their investigations and relate their story to the reader. In the novel, it is just one of the devices by which Stoker conveys the contrasts between the civilized, industrial world and the animalistic savagery of Dracula.

5   See Brady, *A Spiral Way*, 21.

6   See Ziegler, "Felix von Luschan als Walzensammler und Förderer des Berliner Phonogramm-Archivs," 132.

7   For a detailed history of the Aboriginal settlement at Coranderrk, see Lydon, *Eye Contact*. Lydon's work presents not only the complex historical events surrounding the settlement but also the settlers' responses to and perspectives on how they were treated and studied by others.

8   See Smith, "I Would Like to Study Some Problems of Heredity," 141.

9   This episode is the subject of Rowlands and Freedman, "Enemy Professors."

10 The word *corroboree* itself is a European invention, used to describe a wide range of dance ceremonies that could have sacred or theatrical intent. Modern Aboriginal society has long since appropriated the term and applied it equally broadly. Because corroborees have a precise structure, the performances themselves require an enormous amount of skill and practice.

11 Lydon, *Eye Contact*, 198–199.

12 Hart and Pilling, *The Tiwi of North Australia*.

13 Goodale, "The Tiwi Dance for the Dead."

14 Ibid.

15 Ibid., 5–6.

16 Ibid., 9.

17 Hart and Pilling, *The Tiwi of North Australia*, 113.

18 Goodale, "The Tiwi Dance for the Dead," 13.

19 Bleakley, who had been a deputy chief protector from 1911, became the chief protector of Queensland Aborigines in 1914. He held this position until 1942. See J. W. Bleakley, introduction to *The Aborigines of Australia*.

20 Ibid., 214–215.

21 Nelson's website for *Before They Pass Away*, http://www.beforethey.com.

22 Bhabha, *The Location of Culture*, 121, quoting from Jacques Lacan, *Of the Gaze* (London: Hogarth Press, 1977), 99.

23 Ibid., 86 (emphasis in original).

24 Ibid.

25 Eco, *Serendipities*, 54.

26 Ibid.

27 See Newell, "Collecting from the Collectors," 43.

28 See Balfour, "On the Methods Employed by Natives of N.W. Australia," 65.

Appendix A
"What the Tongans Say about Napoleon"

_____

There is no people on the face of the earth so great and noble as are we, the people of Tonga. Other nations may be more numerous and richer, and perhaps even stronger than we; but with us is the root of greatness and with us alone. From our stock has sprung the race of warriors—men whose names are known—some whose mighty deeds have been done among our own people, and others who have lived and fought among foreign nations.

Thus, Napoleoni was a son of Tonga; for his mother came to us in a ship from the land of Merikei (America), which stayed with us for many days hunting whales. She was a young woman, tall and fair; and after a while, she sailed again to her own land, where she brought forth a child, though no man had her to wife, and this child she called Napoleoni.

Now, after many days, when he was grown, the men of Faranise (France) sent ambassadors to Merikei, begging to help against Uelingtoni [Duke of Wellington], who had beaten them in many battles, killing their king, and all the sons of the chiefs. For the high-priest had told them there they would find the child of a red father who would lead them against their enemies, and before whose face no man should be able to stand. So they came sailing over the waters to Merikei in search of him who should lead them to victory; and a weary search they had, for the people mocked them as they went from town to town asking for the son of a red father. The boys followed them, crying aloud, "We are the sons of red fathers. Take us, that we may gain you the victory." In one town, the name of which we have not been told, the young men deceived them shamefully, promising to lead them to the deliverer of their people. And their souls rejoiced.

"Good is our coming," they said to one another. "Good is our coming, for here our troubles end. Woe now to Uelingtoni!"

"True!" said the young men; "your troubles are over, and woe to Uelingtoni. But come now, why do we linger here?" And, leading them through the gateway in the war-fence at the back of the town, and across the moat, they took them to a house in the forest where the farmer lived—for you must know that in

Merikei the husbandmen are not permitted to dwell within the town—and there they showed the men of Faranise a calf! "Here now," they said, "is he whom you seek, for his father is red."

The men of Faranise turned, and went sorrowfully on their way, while the mocking laughter of the cruel youths sounded in their ears. But toward evening they came to a little house, standing by itself in the midst of the wood; and in this house dwelt the mother of Napoleoni.

"Let us ask here also," said the chief man among them. "It may be that we shall yet find him; for surely the high-priest could not have lied to us, and his words were that we should find our deliverer in this land. Therefore let us ask here also."

So they made their inquiry; and the mother of Napoleoni cried aloud in wonder when she heard their words. "Who then are you?" she cried. "Who told you that the father of my son is red?"

"We are chiefs," they replied. "From the land of Faranise we come. We are seeking the child of a red father, who is to save us from our enemy Uelingtoni, and revenge all the evils he has brought upon our people. We were sent by our great priest, who told us that here we should find the deliverer of our people, the son of a man whose skin is red."

The woman stood, gasping with wonder. "Truly the gods have sent you," she cried. "I have a son whose father is a chief in Tonga. But this is my son—he who is sitting there on the mat—he is dumb. How then can he be the leader of your people?"

Never before had Napoleoni spoken; he had been dumb from the day of his birth; but now he rose and spake, for his time was come. Tall and strong—taller than the tallest of the strangers—he rose from the floor-mat on which he had been sitting.

"I am he whom you seek," he said. "Come! Let us go to your canoe and sail, that I may lead you to victory. Farewell, my mother! Be of good cheer, for I shall come again in triumph, when I have smitten the enemy of these our friends. Or if I come not again, I will send for you to the land where it shall please me to dwell."

"Farewell, my son," said his mother, following him to the door, and plucking a flower that grew near by. "Go, and may the gods be your helpers! Take this flower; and when you look upon it, think then of your father and of me."

The flower which she gave him was red.

So he led the men of Faranise. I could tell you of his mighty deeds—how he smote the enemies of Faranise, though they were many and strong; how he chased Uelingtoni from land to land, till he caught him at Uatalu [Waterloo], and banished him to a desert island, where he died.

Of all these things I could tell you; but to what end? All the world knows them. But of his birth only, and his going to Faranise, have I told you, because the men of Faranise hide the truth, giving out that he was truly one of themselves, born in an island, the dwelling-place of their royal clan. This lie they tell, envying us, the people of Tonga, because of our greatness. The men of Merikei also claim him, because they have red-skinned men among them; but the truth is that which I have told you here to-day. I am Vave of Kolonga.

Notes

This tale is presented verbatim, as it is recorded in Fison, *Tales of Old Fiji*, 135–138.

Appendix B
Exhibition Object List

Cat. 1
Munkiai (globular whistle)
Bongu culture, Rai Coast,
Papua New Guinea
Late 19th century
Nut shell, thread; cardboard, ink on paper,
copper alloy
1¾ × 1⅝ in. (4.5 × 4 cm); board: 3⅜ × 3⅜ in.
(8.5 × 8.5 cm)
Division of Anthropology, American
Museum of Natural History, ST/ 676

Cat. 2
Monitor lizard skin for drumhead
Finschhafen, Madang Province,
Papua New Guinea
Late 19th century
Monitor lizard skin; cardboard, ink on paper
8½ × 6⅝ × ¼ in. (21.5 × 16.7 × 0.8 cm);
board: 8¾ × 9⅛ in. (22 × 23 cm)
Division of Anthropology, American
Museum of Natural History, ST/ 648
See Fig. 4

Cat. 3
Tatanua (mask for funerary ceremony)
Malagan culture, New Ireland, Nusa Island,
Papua New Guinea
Late 19th century
Wood, shell, pigment, plant fiber, seed,
resin, bark cloth, paper
19¼ × 11 × 6¼ in. (49 × 28 × 16 cm)
Division of Anthropology, American
Museum of Natural History, ST/ 691
See Fig. 11

Cat. 4
Lower jaw of shark
Nukumanu Atoll, Papua New Guinea
Late 19th century
Shark jaw, cartilage and teeth
9⅜ × 7⅛ × 2¾ in. (24 × 18 × 7 cm)
Division of Anthropology, American
Museum of Natural History, ST/ 754

Cat. 5
Skate skin used as a spear sheath
I-Kiribati culture, Tarawa, Kiribati
Late 19th century
Skate skin
8⁷⁄₈ × 2¹⁄₈ × 1³⁄₄ in. (22.5 × 5.3 × 4.5 cm)
Division of Anthropology, American
Museum of Natural History, ST/ 758 AB
See Fig. 12

Cat. 6
Boomerang
Queensland, Australia
Late 19th century
Wood, pigment
25¹⁄₄ × 2³⁄₈ × ⁵⁄₈ in. (64 × 6 × 1.5 cm)
Division of Anthropology, American
Museum of Natural History, ST/ 764
See Fig. 14

Cat. 7
Hand club
Massim, Papua New Guinea
Late 19th century
Wood, pigment
20³⁄₄ × 2¹⁄₄ × ³⁄₄ in. (52.5 × 5.5 × 2 cm)
Division of Anthropology, American
Museum of Natural History, ST/ 850
See Fig. 13

Cat. 8
Red loam sample
Motu culture, Port Moresby,
Papua New Guinea
Late 19th century
Glass, loam; metal wire, thread, ink on
paper
5¹⁄₂ × 2⁵⁄₈ in. (14 × 6.5 cm)
Division of Anthropology, American
Museum of Natural History, ST/1052
See Fig. 7

Cat. 9
Dark loam sample
Motu culture, Port Moresby,
Papua New Guinea
Late 19th century
Iron alloy, loam; ink on paper
4¹⁄₂ × 3 in. (11.5 × 7.5 cm)
Division of Anthropology, American
Museum of Natural History, ST/1050

Cat. 10
Fishhooks (Aibo)
Matupi culture, Matupi Island, New Britain,
Papua New Guinea
Late 19th century
Plant fiber, fish spine; cardboard, copper
alloy, ink on paper
Board: 11 × 4⁷⁄₈ in. (28 × 12.5 cm)
Division of Anthropology, American
Museum of Natural History, ST/ 946
See Fig. 15

Cat. 11
Water vessel
Admiralty Islands, Papua New Guinea
Late 19th century
Coconut shell, plant fiber thread, dye
18¹⁄₈ × 3⁷⁄₈ in. (46 × 10 cm)
Division of Anthropology, American
Museum of Natural History, ST/1025
See Fig. 16

Cat. 12
Headrest
Finschhafen, Madang Province,
Papua New Guinea
Late 19th century
Wood, traces of pigment or dirt
6 × 2⅛ × 6⅞ in. (15.3 × 5.3 × 17.5 cm)
Division of Anthropology, American
Museum of Natural History, ST/1090
See Fig. 5

Cat. 13
Bilum (pack net)
Motu culture, Port Moresby,
Papua New Guinea
Late 19th century
Plant fiber thread, dye; ink on paper
13 × 5⅞ in. (33 × 15 cm)
Division of Anthropology, American
Museum of Natural History, ST/1385
See Fig. 8

Cat. 14
Axe with handle
Kaile, Papua New Guinea
Late 19th century
Stone, wood, plant fiber thread
16⅛ × 11⅜ × 4¼ in (41 × 29 × 11 cm);
blade: 9⅛ × 4¼ × ¾ in. (23 × 11 × 2 cm)
Division of Anthropology, American
Museum of Natural History, ST/1133 A-E
See Fig. 17

Cat. 15
Fur pelt
Venus Point, Madang Province,
Papua New Guinea
Late 19th century
Fur; cardboard, ink on paper
Board: 8½ × 7¼ × ¾ in. (20.5 × 18.5 × 2 cm)
Division of Anthropology, American
Museum of Natural History, ST/1898

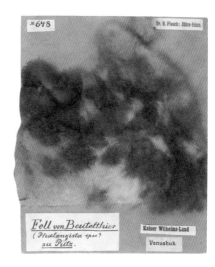

Cat. 16
Feathers
Astrolabe Mountains, Papua New Guinea
Late 19th century
Eclectus parrot feathers; cardboard, ink on
paper, string, copper alloy
Board: 8⅞ × 11 in. (22.5 × 28 cm)
Division of Anthropology, American
Museum of Natural History, ST/1945 A–F
See Fig. 6

Cat. 17
Canoe head carving
Vanimo culture, Angriffshafen,
Papua New Guinea
Late 19th century
Wood, pigment
22¾ × 5⅞ × 1⅝ in. (58 × 15 × 4 cm)
Division of Anthropology, American
Museum of Natural History, ST/1093
See Fig. 9

Cat. 18
War club
Ni-Vanuatu culture, Ambrym Island,
Vanuatu
Late 19th century
Wood
45¾ × 10⅜ × 3⅛ in. (116 × 26.5 × 8 cm)
Division of Anthropology, American
Museum of Natural History, 80.0/ 696

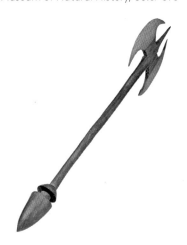

Cat. 19
Cutlass-shaped club
Papua New Guinea
Early 20th century
Wood, pigment; ink on paper, graphite
28¼ × 3⅛ × 1¼ in. (72 × 8 × 3 cm)
Division of Anthropology, American
Museum of Natural History, 80.0/4349

Cat. 20
Cutlass-shaped club
Trobriand Islands, Massim,
Papua New Guinea
Early 20th century
Wood, pigment
28¼ × 3½ × 1 in. (72 × 9 × 2.5 cm)
Division of Anthropology, American
Museum of Natural History, 80.0/9903
See Fig. 1

Cat. 21
Pipe
Arunta culture, Central Australia,
Northern Territory, Australia
Late 19th century
Wood, pigment; metal, plant fiber, soot
25⅝ × 1⅝ × 1¼ in. (65 × 4 × 3 cm)
Division of Anthropology, American
Museum of Natural History, ST/4179
See Fig. 26

Cat. 22
Pipe
Yolngu culture, Elcho Island, Arnhem Land,
Northern Territory, Australia
Mid-20th century
Wood, pigment; metal, soot
9⅜ × 1⅝ × 2¾ in. (24 × 4 × 7 cm)
Division of Anthropology, American
Museum of Natural History, 80.1/3670
See Fig. 27

Cat. 23
Child's imitation pipe
Arapesh culture, Aitape district,
Papua New Guinea
Early 20th century
Reed wood
3½ × 2¾ × ¾ in. (9 × 7 × 2 cm)
Division of Anthropology, American
Museum of Natural History, 80.0/6981
See Fig. 30

Cat. 24
Kauri heart
Auckland, New Zealand
Late 19th century
Gum (Kauri tree); velvet case, silk satin
1¾ × 1⅜ × ⅝ in. (4.5 × 3.5 × 1.6 cm)
Division of Anthropology, American
Museum of Natural History, 80.0/4110 A–C

Cat. 25
Bottle glass fragment
Laverton Reserve, Western Australia,
Australia
Late 20th century
Green bottle glass
2⅜ × 2 × 1 in. (6 × 5 × 2.5 cm)
Division of Anthropology, American
Museum of Natural History, 80.1/4871 A

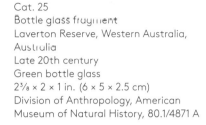

Cat. 26
Adze
Kanak culture, New Caledonia
Late 19th century
Stone, wood, cotton, fur, plant fiber cord,
coconut husk
25 × 12¾ × 3⅝ in. (63.5 × 32.5 × 9.2 cm)
Division of Anthropology, American
Museum of Natural History, 80.0/ 763

Cat. 27
Civavonovono, or *civitabua* (breastplate)
Fiji
Late 19th century
Pearl oyster shell, sperm whale tooth, white
metal, plant fiber
13¾ × 8¼ × 1⅜ in. (35 × 20.9 × 3.6 cm)
Division of Anthropology, American
Museum of Natural History, 80.0/2061.
See Fig. 21

Cat. 28
Civavonovono, or *civitabua* (breastplate)
Fiji
Late 19th century
Pearl oyster shell, sperm whale tooth, white
metal, plant fiber
13¾ × 9¼ × 1¼ in. (35 × 23 × 3 cm)
Division of Anthropology, American
Museum of Natural History, 80.0/2062
See Fig. 21

Cat. 29
Woman's bonnet
Ni-Vanuatu culture, Aneityum, Vanuatu
Late 19th century
Pandanus leaf, cotton, silk ribbon,
newspaper
21¼ × 9⅜ × ¾ in. (54 × 24 × 2 cm)
Division of Anthropology, American
Museum of Natural History, ST/3267
See Figs. 32, 33

Cat. 30
*Gov. Arthur's Proclamation to the
Tasmanian Peoples*
Tasmania, Australia
1830
Oil on wood panel
13⅛ × 8⅞ × ⅜ in. (33.1 × 22.5 × 0.9 cm)
Museum Purchase © President and Fellows
of Harvard College, Peabody Museum of
Archaeology and Ethnology, PM 72-21-70 /
6500 (digital file #60743328)

Cat. 31
Walking stick curio
Halls Creek, Kimberley region,
Western Australia, Australia
1918
Wood, heat-applied incising.
34 × 7¼ × 1¾ in. (86.3 × 18.5 × 4.3 cm)
Museum Purchase © President and Fellows
of Harvard College, Peabody Museum of
Archaeology and Ethnology, PM 32-68-70 /
D3946 (digital file #99270004)

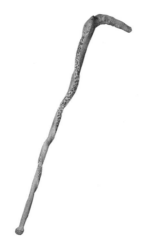

Cat. 32
Commemoration shield
Forest River, Kimberley region,
Western Australia, Australia
Early 20th century
Wood, pigment
39⅜ × 7½ in. (11 × 19 cm)
University of Pennsylvania, Museum
of Archaeology and Anthropology,
Philadelphia, PA 31-33-6

Cat. 33, Cat. 34, and Cat. 35
Glass points
Murchison district, Kimberley region,
Western Australia, Australia
1908
Glass
5¾ × 1⅜ × ¼ in. (14.8 × 3.6 × 0.7 cm);
5¼ × 1¼ × ¼ in. (13.2 × 3.2 × 0.7 cm);
3¾ × 3½ × ¼ in. (9.6 × 3.5 × 0.6 cm)
University of Pennsylvania Museum
of Archaeology and Anthropology,
Philadelphia, PA, 31-33-101, 31-33-104,
31-33-113
See Fig. 24

Cat. 36 and Cat. 37
Ceramic points
Forest River, Kimberley region,
Western Australia, Australia;
Murchison district, Kimberley region,
Western Australia, Australia
1906
Porcelain
4⅛ × ⅞ × ¼ in. (10.5 × 2.4 × 0.5 cm);
2⅞ × ⅞ × ¼ in. (7.4 × 2.3 × 0.5 cm)
University of Pennsylvania Museum of
Archaeology and Anthropology,
31-33-116 and 31-33-76
See Fig. 25

Cat. 38
Pukumani, or Tutini (Tiwi mortuary pole)
Tiwi culture, Melville Island, Northern
Territory, Australia
1954
Wood, pigment
83 × 11¾ × 11¾ in. (211 × 30 × 30 cm)
University of Pennsylvania, Museum of
Archaeology and Anthropology, 55-17-2

Cat. 39
Tahi'i (fan)
Marquesas Islands, French Polynesia
19th century
Plant fiber, wood
13¼ × 11⅜ × ¾ in. (33.7 × 28.9 × 1.9 cm)
Brooklyn Museum, by exchange, 42.243.2

Bibliography

Aird, Michael. "Growing Up with Aborigines." In *Photography's Other Histories*, edited by Christopher Pinney and Nicolas Peterson, 23–39. Durham, NC: Duke University Press, 2003.

Akerman, Kim. "On Kimberley Points and the Politics of Enchantment." *Current Anthropology* 48, no. 1 (February 2007): 133–134.

Anderson, Benedict. *Imagined Communities: Reflections on the Origin and Spread of Nationalism.* London: Verso, 1993.

Anonymous. "Geography and Travels." *American Naturalist* 17, no. 2 (February 1883): 185–189.

Appadurai, Arjun. *The Social Life of Things: Commodities in Cultural Perspective.* Cambridge: Cambridge University Press, 1986.

Ashcroft, Bill, Gareth Griffiths, and Helen Tiffin. *Key Concepts in Post-Colonial Studies.* New York: Routledge, 1998.

Balfour, Henry. *The Evolution of Decorative Art: An Essay upon Its Origin and Development as Illustrated by the Art of Modern Races of Mankind.* New York: Macmillan, 1893.

———. "On the Methods Employed by Natives of N.W. Australia in the Manufacture of Glass Spear Heads." *Man* 1, no. 5 (1903): 65.

Basedow, Herbert. *The Australian Aboriginal.* Adelaide: F. W. Preece, 1925.

Baudrillard, Jean. "The Precession of Simulacra." In *Simulacra and Simulation*, trans. Sheila Faria Glaser, 1–15. Ann Arbor: University of Michigan Press, 1994.

Bhabha, Homi. *The Location of Culture.* London: Routledge, 1994.

Bleakley, J. W. *The Aborigines of Australia.* Brisbane: Jacaranda Press, 1961.

Bolton, Lissant. "Gender, Status and Introduced Clothing in Vanuatu." In *Clothing the Pacific*, edited by Chloe Colchester, 119–139. Oxford: Berg, 2003.

Brady, Erica. *A Spiral Way: How the Phonograph Changed Ethnography.* Jackson: University Press of Mississippi, 1999.

Buschmann, Rainer. *Anthropology's Global Histories: The Ethnographic Frontier in German New Guinea 1870–1935.* Honolulu: University of Hawai'i Press, 2009.

———. "Uncertain Currents: German Ethnographic Perspectives on the 18th and 19th Century Pacific." Paper delivered at the 10th Conference of the European Society for Oceanists, Brussels, June 2015.

Butcher, Barry. "Darwinism, Social Darwinism, and the Australian Aborigines: A Re-Evaluation." In *Darwin's Laboratory: Evolutionary Theory and Natural History in the Pacific*, edited by Roy Macleod and Philip F. Rehbock, 371–394. Honolulu: University of Hawai'i Press, 1994.

Casey, Maryrose. "Colonisation, Notions of Authenticity and Aboriginal Australian Performance." *Critical Race and Whiteness Studies* 8 (2012): 6–18.

Castillo, Susan. "'The Best of Nations'? Race and Imperial Destiny in Emerson's 'English Traits.'" *Yearbook of English Studies* 34 (2004): 100–111.

Cleland, W. L. "President's Address." *Transactions and Proceedings and Report of the Royal Society of South Australia* 23 (1898–1899): 306–307.

Danaiyarri, Hobbles. "The Saga of Captain Cook 1." In *Australia's Empire*, edited by Deryck M. Schreuder and Stuart Ward, 27–32. Oxford: Oxford University Press, 2008.

Daniel, Glyn, and Colin Renfrew. *The Idea of Prehistory.* Edinburgh: Edinburgh University Press, 1988.

Deniker, Joseph. *The Races of Man: An Outline of Anthropology and Ethnography.* London: Walter Scott, 1900.

Denoon, Donald, Malama Meleisea, Stewart Firth, and Jocelyn Linnekin. *The Cambridge History of the Pacific Islanders.* Cambridge: Cambridge University Press, 1997.

Disraeli, Benjamin. *Tancred*, London; R. Brimley Johnson, 1904. Originally published in 1847.

Douglas, Bronwen, and Chris Ballard, eds. *Foreign Bodies: Oceania and the Science of Race 1750–1940*. Canberra: ANU E Press, 2010.

Eco, Umberto. *Serendipities*. New York: Columbia University Press, 1998.

Eliot, T. S. "Tradition and the Individual Talent." In *Selected Essays*, 3–11. London: Faber and Faber, 1951.

Elkin, A. P. "Conservation of Aboriginal Peoples Whose Modes of Life Are of Scientific Interest." *Man* 46 (1946): 94–96.

——. "Pressure Flaking in Northern Kimberley, Australia." *Man* 48 (1948): 110–113.

Etheridge, R. "On Some Beautifully-Formed Stone Spear-Heads, from Kimberley, North-West Australia." *Records of the Geological Survey of New South Wales* 11, no. 2 (1890): 61–65.

Finsch, Otto. *Ethnologischer Atlas: Typen aus der Steinzeit Neu-Guineas*. Translated by H. Soltmann. Leipzig: Ferdinand Hirt, 1888. English text translated by T. Symonds.

Fison, Lorimer. *Tales of Old Fiji*. London: Alexander Moring, 1904.

Fison, Lorimer, and A. W. Howitt. *Kamilaroi and Kurnai: Group Marriage and Relationship, and Marriage by Elopement*. Melbourne: George Robertson, 1880. Reprint, Canberra: Aboriginal Studies Press, 1991.

Frame, Tom. *Evolution in the Antipodes: Charles Darwin and Australia*. Sydney: University of New South Wales Press, 2009.

Ganter, Regina. "WE Roth on Asians in Australia." In *The Roth Family, Anthropology, and Colonial Administration*, edited by Iain Davidson and Russell McDougall, 157–170. Walnut Creek, CA: Left Coast Press, 2008.

Ganter, Regina, and Ross Kidd. "The Power of Protectors: Conflicts Surrounding Queensland's 1897 Aboriginal Legislation." *Australian Historical Studies*, no. 101 (October 1993): 536–554.

Goodale, Jane. "The Tiwi Dance for the Dead." *Expedition* 2, no. 1 (September 1959): 3–13.

Gould, Stephen J. *The Mismeasure of Man*. New York: Norton, 1996.

Griffiths, Thomas. *Hunters and Collectors*. Cambridge: Cambridge University Press, 1996.

Gross, David. *The Past in Ruins: Tradition and the Critique of Modernity*. Amherst: University of Massachusetts Press, 1992.

Hardman, Edward T. "Notes on a Collection of Native Weapons and Implements from Tropical Western Australia (Kimberley District)." *Proceedings of the Royal Irish Academy*, 3d ser., vol. 1 (1889–1891): 57–69.

Harrison, Rodney. "An Artefact of Colonial Desire? Kimberley Points and the Technologies of Enchantment." *Current Anthropology* 47, no. 1 (February 2006): 63–88.

——. "'The Magical Virtue of These Sharp Things': Colonialism, Mimesis and Knapped Bottle Glass Artefacts in Australia." *Journal of Material Culture* 8, no. 3: 311–336.

Hart, C. M. W., and Arnold R. Pilling. *The Tiwi of North Australia*. New York: Holt, Rinehart, and Winston, 1960.

Healy, J. J. "Literature, Power and the Refusals of Big Bear: Reflection on the Treatment of the Indian and the Aborigine." In *Australian/Canadian Literatures in English: Comparative Perspectives*, edited by Russell McDougall and Gillian Whitlock, 66–93. North Ryde, New South Wales: Methuen Australia, 1987.

Hempenstall, Peter J. *Pacific Islanders under German Rule: A Study in the Meaning of Colonial Resistance*. Canberra: Australian National University Press, 1978.

Herle, Anita, and Lucie Carreau. *Chiefs and Governors: Art and Power in Fiji*. Cambridge: Museum of Archaeology and Anthropology, University of Cambridge, 2014.

Hobsbawm, Eric. Introduction to *The Invention of Tradition*, edited by Eric Hobsbawm and Terence Ranger, 1–14. Cambridge: Cambridge University Press, 2004.

Hodder, Ian. *Entangled: An Archaeology of the Relationship between Humans and Things*. London: Wiley-Blackwell, 2012.

Horsman, Reginald. "Origins of Racial Anglo-Saxonism in Great Britain before 1850." *Journal of the History of Ideas* 37, no. 3 (July–September 1976): 387–410.

Howes, Hilary. *Germanica Pacifica: The Race Question in Oceania; A. B. Meyer and Otto Finsch between Metropolitan Theory and Field Experience, 1865–1914*. Frankfurt: Peter Lang, 2013.

———. "'It Is Not So!': Otto Finsch, Expectations and Encounters in the Pacific, 1865–1885." *Historical Records of Australian Science* 22 (2001): 32–52.

Igler, David. "Exploring the Concept of Empire in Pacific History: Individuals, Nations, and Ocean Space Prior to 1850." *History Compass* 12, no. 1 (November 2014): 879–887.

Khan, Kate. *Catalogue of the Roth Collection of Aboriginal Artefacts from North Queensland*, vol. 1. Sydney: Australian Museum, 1993.

Knox, Robert. *The Races of Men: A Philosophical Enquiry into the Influence of Race over the Destinies of Nations*. London: Beaufort, 1850.

Lorimer, Douglas A. "Race, Science and Culture: Historical Continuities and Discontinuities, 1850–1914." In *The Victorians and Race*, edited by Shearer West, 12–33. Aldershot, UK: Ashgate, 1996.

Lydon, Jane. *Eye Contact: Photographing Indigenous Australians*. Durham, NC: Duke University Press, 2005.

Macleod, Roy, and Philip F. Rehbock, eds. *Darwin's Laboratory: Evolutionary Theory and Natural History in the Pacific*. Honolulu: University of Hawai'i Press, 1994.

Martin, Calvin. "The European Impact on the Culture of a Northeastern Algonquian Tribe: An Ecological Interpretation." *William and Mary Quarterly* 31, no. 1 (1974): 3–26.

McGregor, Russell. "The Doomed Race: A Scientific Axiom of the Late Nineteenth Century." *Australian Journal of Politics and History* 39 (1993): 14–22.

Meston, Archibald. "The Evolution of the Boomerang: Part I." *Steele Rudd's Magazine* (April 1905): 365–370.

———. *Report on the Aboriginals of Queensland*. Canberra: National Library of Australia, 1896.

Mortensen, Reid. "Slaving in Australian Courts: Blackbirding Cases, 1869–1871." *Journal of South Pacific Law* 13, no. 1 (2009): 7–37.

Mulvaney, John. "'Annexing All I Can Lay Hands On': Baldwin Spencer as Ethnographic Collector." In *The Makers and Making of Indigenous Australian Museum Collections*, edited by N. Peterson, L. Allen, and L. Hamley, 107–120. Melbourne: Melbourne University Press, 2008.

Neich, Roger, and Fuli Pereira. *Pacific Jewelry and Adornment*. Honolulu: University of Hawai'i Press, 2004.

Nelson, Jimmy. *Before They Pass Away*. Kempen, Germany: teNeues, 2013.

Newell, Jenny. "Collecting from the Collectors: Pacific Islanders and the Spoils of Europe." In *Cook's Pacific Encounters: The Cook-Forster Collection of the Georg-August University of Göttingen*, edited by Therese Weber and Jeanie Watson, 29–47. Canberra: National Museum of Australia, 2006.

Noble, William, and Iain Davidson. *Human Evolution, Language and Mind: A Psychological and Archaeological Inquiry*. Cambridge: Cambridge University Press, 1996.

Osborn, Henry Fairfield. *History, Plan and Scope of the American Museum of Natural History: Preliminary Report Printed for the Forty-First Annual Meeting of the Trustees February 14, 1910*. New York: Irving Press, 1910.

Pearce, S. M. "Collecting Reconsidered." In *Interpreting Objects and Collections*, edited by S. M. Pearce, 193–204. London: Routledge, 1994.

Pels, Peter. "The Anthropology of Colonialism: Culture, History, and the Emergence of Western Governmentality." *Annual Review of Anthropology* 26 (1997): 163–183.

Penny, H. Glen. *Objects of Culture: Ethnology and Ethnographic Museums in Imperial Germany*. Chapel Hill: University of North Carolina Press, 2002.

Pike, Glenvllle. "The Northern Territory Overland Telegraph: An Epic of Courage—Just 100 Years Ago." *Journal of the Royal Historical Society of Queensland* 9, no. 2 (1971): 95–133.

Pratt, Mary Louise. *Imperial Eyes: Travel Writing and Transculturation.* New York: Routledge, 1992.

Prown, Jules David. "In Pursuit of Culture: The Formal Language of Objects." *American Art* 9, no. 2 (Summer 1995): 2–3.

Reynolds, B. "Australian Material Culture: Handbook of Aboriginal and Torres Strait Islander Material Cultures, Vol. 1: Northeast." Unpublished MS.

Richardson, Ruth. *Death, Dissection and the Destitute.* London: Kegan Paul, 1987.

Roberts, David Andrew. "The Frontier." In *High Lean Country: Land, People and Memory in New England*, edited by Alan Atkinson, J. S. Ryan, Iain Davidson, and Andrew Piper, 98–110. Crow's Nest, New South Wales: Allen and Unwin, 2006.

Robertson, H. A. *Erromanga, the Martyr Isle.* London: Hodder and Stoughton, 1902.

Rosaldo, Renato. "Imperialist Nostalgia." "Memory and Counter Memory," special issue, *Representations*, no. 26 (Spring 1989): 107–122.

Roth, Henry Ling. *The Aborigines of Tasmania.* London: Kegan Paul, 1890. Reprint, Hobart, Tasmania: Fullers Bookshop, 1968.

———. "On the Use and Display of Anthropological Collections in Museums." *Museums Journal* 10 (1911): 286–290.

Roth, Walter Edmund. *Ethnological Studies among the North-West-Central Queensland Aborigines.* Brisbane: Government Printer, 1897.

Rowlands, Shawn C., and Catriona Fisk. "Broken Glass: Craft, Industry, and Aboriginal Material Culture in Early Twentieth-Century Australia." Paper presented at the Fourth Annual Stickley Museum at Craftsman Farms Emerging Scholars Symposium, Morris Plains, NJ, October 2014.

———. "'A Dearly Bought Amusement': Race, Punishment, and Resistance on Australia's Telegraph Lines." Paper presented at the Conference on Hunting and Gathering Societies, Vienna, September 2015.

Rowlands, Shawn C., and Erin Alexa Freedman. "Enemy Professors." Paper delivered at the 10th Conference of the European Society for Oceanists, Brussels, June 2015.

Rowlands, Shawn C., and Sergio Jarillo de la Torre. "Not by Blood, but Some Iron: Otto Finsch's Ethnographic Imperialism in Oceania, and the Ways of Indigenous Resistance." Paper delivered at the 10th Conference of the European Society for Oceanists, Brussels, June 2015.

Rowse, Tim. *White Flour, White Power: From Relations to Citizenship in Central Australia.* Cambridge: Cambridge University Press, 1998.

Said, Edward. *Orientalism.* London: Penguin, 2003.

Scott, Ernest. *A Short History of Australia.* London: Oxford University Press, 1929. Originally published in 1916.

Scott, James C. *Domination and the Arts of Resistance: Hidden Transcripts.* New Haven, CT: Yale University Press, 1990.

Seed, David. "Nineteenth-Century Travel Writing: An Introduction." *Yearbook of English Studies* 34 (2004): 1–5.

Silliman, Stephen W. "Disentangling the Archaeology of Colonialism and Indigeneity." In *Archaeology of Entanglement*, edited by Lindsay Der and Francesca Fernandini, chap. 1. Walnut Creek, CA: Left Coast Press, 2015.

Smith, John David. "'I Would Like to Study Some Problems of Heredity': Felix von Luschan's Trip to America, 1914–1915." In *Felix von Luschan (1854–1924): Leben und Wirken eines Universalgelehrten*, edited by Peter Ruggendorfer and Hubert D. Szemethy, 141–163. Vienna: Böhlau, 2009.

Spencer, W. Baldwin, and F. J. Gillen. *The Native Tribes of Central Australia.* London: Macmillan, 1899. Reprint, Cambridge: Cambridge University Press, 2010.

Spurr, David. *The Rhetoric of Empire: Colonial Discourse in Journalism, Travel Writing, and Imperial Administration.* Durham, NC: Duke University Press, 1993.

Steel, Robert. *The New Hebrides and Christian Missions: With a Sketch of the Labour Traffic and Notes of a Cruise through the Group in the Mission Vessel.* London: James Nisbet, 1880.

Stocking, George W., Jr. *Race, Culture, and Evolution: Essays in the History of Anthropology.* New York: Free Press, 1968.

Tapsell, Paul. "(Post)musings from the Edge: Being an Indigenous Curator in Pacific Paradise." Paper presented at the Indigenous Arts in Transition Seminar, Bard Graduate Center, New York, May 6, 2015.

Taussig, M. *Mimesis and Alterity: A Particular History of the Senses.* New York: Routledge, 1993.

Taylor, Cheryl. "Constructing Aboriginality: Archibald Meston's Literary Journalism, 1870–1924." *Journal of the Association for the Study of Australian Literature* 2 (2003): 121–139.

Thomas, Nicholas. *Colonialism's Culture: Anthropology, Travel and Government.* Princeton, NJ: Princeton University Press, 1994.

———. *Entangled Objects: Exchange, Material Culture, and Colonialism in the Pacific.* Cambridge, MA: Harvard University Press, 1991.

Turner, Frederick Jackson. *Frontier and Section: Selected Essays of Frederick Jackson Turner.* Edited by Ray Allen Billington. Englewood Cliffs, NJ: Prentice-Hall, 1961.

Tylor, E. B. *Primitive Culture: Researches into the Development of Mythology, Philosophy, Religion, Language, Art and Custom.* London: Murray, 1891.

Wiessner, Polly. "Style and Changing Relations between the Individual and Society." In *The Meaning of Things*, edited by Ian Hodder, 56–64. London: Unwin Hyman, 1989.

Wilson, H. T. *Tradition and Innovation: The Idea of Civilization as Culture and Its Significance.* London: Routledge and Kegan Paul, 1984.

Ziegler, Susanne. "Felix von Luschan als Walzensammler und Förderer des Berliner Phonogramm-Archivs." In *Felix von Luschan (1854–1924): Leben und Wirken eines Universalgelehrten*, edited by Peter Ruggendorfer and Hubert D. Szemethy. Vienna: Böhlau, 2009.

Index

Italic page numbers indicate illustrations.